YOU ARE A
STRATEGIST

USE NO-BS OKRs
TO GET BIG THINGS DONE

SARA LOBKOVICH

Published by Red Currant Collective LLC

Connected Strategic®, Evolutionary OKRs®, and Thinkydoers® are registered trademarks of Red Currant Collective LLC. No-BS OKRs™ and Rebelutionary™ are trademarks of Red Currant Collective LLC (registration pending).

Printed in the United States of America

ISBN (Ebook): 979-8-9908066-2-7
ISBN (Paperback): 979-8-9908066-1-0
ISBN (Hardback): 979-8-9908066-0-3
ISBN (Audiobook): 979-8-9908066-3-4

Edited by Laura Matthews, www.thinkStory.biz
Cover and interior design and typesetting by Caerus Kourt

First Edition

This book is dedicated to introverted, neurodivergent, queer, and historically marginalized people; to square pegs, frustrated changemakers, Rebelutionaries, and Thinkydoers. To everyone who's ever heard the words, "You need to be more strategic," or "You're overcomplicating this."

You are not alone, and together, we can change the world.

"What would happen if you stopped worrying about whether others understood your value, and simply brought that value to the work itself? What would be different if you stopped waiting for permission?"

Sara Wachter-Boettcher

CONTENTS

FOREWORD

BY CINDY (WHITE) SHEA

In the ever-evolving landscape of business and innovation, the quest for clarity and impact often feels like navigating a labyrinth. Many leaders and team members have faced the frustration of being told to "be more strategic" or to "simplify things," only to be left with more questions than answers.

I was one of those people—driven, passionate, and eager to make a difference—yet I was often caught in the crossfire of well-intentioned but confusing advice from senior leaders. As a career strategic project management professional currently serving as the VP of Operational Excellence at both Pearson Virtual Schools and Higher Education Divisions, I have been responsible for developing and executing the vision and operating model for enterprise planning. In my journey in strategic enterprise planning, I had implemented various versions of goal setting processes, but it wasn't until I took a class on OKR coaching taught by this book's author, Sara Lobkovich, that the lightbulb turned on. Sara's method didn't just change the way I approached my work; it revolutionized it.

For example, Sara helped me shift my perspective to think more strategically with an execution focus. During a particularly challenging phase of our company's subsequent OKR journey, with Sara as our consultant, she reminded me to be curious and to metaphorically change my hat from that of an employee to someone observing the situation from afar, wondering why things were unfolding the way they were.

This kind of advice was transformative for me. It not only helped me develop a stronger sense of self but also significantly improved how I perceived myself as an OKR coach and strategic thinker. By adopting a new mindset, I was able to approach problems with a fresh perspective, leading to more effective solutions and ultimately contributing to the success of the program. Sara's guidance was instrumental in this personal and professional growth.

Sara showed us at Pearson how OKRs can provide a structured yet flexible method to bridge the often daunting gap between high-level strategy and ground-level execution. This allowed me to connect the dots in a way that was both meaningful and actionable, transforming abstract goals into concrete results.

After three years of focused effort, Pearson's Center of Excellence is seeing clear returns from its OKR investment:

- **Strategic clarity.** OKRs now differentiate important goals from ongoing operations. Employees understand top priorities and how their efforts connect.
- **Outcome mindset.** Teams continue to mature in shifting from activity-based goals to measurable outcomes.
- **Cross-functional work.** The breaking down of silos to identify shared objectives has been hugely impactful.
- **Accelerated learning.** Regular progress reviews and retrospectives help teams quickly learn and adjust.

The book in your hands, *You Are a Strategist*, by my OKR mentor Sara Lobkovich, will show you how to get the same results. It is a playbook designed for, as Sara describes it, the rebels and dedicated changemakers among us—those who are not content with the status quo and are always seeking to push the boundaries of what is possible. Whether you're a seasoned leader or an ambitious newcomer, this book offers a no-nonsense approach to harnessing the power of OKRs to amplify your impact.

Inside these pages, you will find practical insights and real-world examples that demystify the OKR process. As you delve deeper into the book, you'll learn how to set audacious yet achievable objectives, define key results that drive progress, and create a culture of accountability and excellence. This is not just another business book filled with abstract theories; it is a hands-on guide from an author with wide experience that equips you with the tools and mindset needed to turn bold visions into reality.

This book will serve as your trusted companion on the journey to achieving extraordinary outcomes—and it is a journey. Embrace the principles and practices outlined here, and you'll find that the path to connecting strategy with implementation is not only navigable but also exhilarating.

Here's to getting big things done.

Cindy (White) Shea
VP, Operational Excellence
Pearson Higher Education
and Virtual Learning Divisions

INTRODUCTION

Think of yourself and those who work for you. How would you all answer these questions?

- Is it important to you [them] for your [their] work to have purpose?
- Are you [they] curious, sometimes to a fault?
- Do you [they] tend to challenge the status quo, in big or little ways?
- Do you [they] intuitively make connections that other people don't?
- Are you [they] comfortable with the risks of intentional experimentation?

If you lead people who would say yes to these questions, you may recognize them as some of your most challenging reports: high potential, perhaps, and also hard to manage.

If you yourself are saying yes to the questions, this could explain why you might be experiencing challenges in your career, especially with authority figures. You may have left jobs (or even been fired) because of a mismatch between your leadership or organizational culture and what you need to feel engaged, empowered, and successful.

You may also have been brought into roles with the promise of innovation and transformation, only to find the organization doesn't really have the appetite, stomach, or culture to make it happen. You may begin each role excited, highly motivated, and sure that *this time will be different*, only to end disillusioned, disappointed, and wondering what you did wrong.

What's running through your head, right now, after reading that?

If you're a leader who is thinking, "How could anyone live like that?" then I'm really glad you're here. A significant percentage of the people you lead or work with live *exactly like that* and need your understanding and support to do their best work. These pages will give you a set of tools to maximize the folks described above as powerful agents of growth, innovation, and transformational change for your organization—*if* you have the stomach for it.

> **It is not just you. We are everywhere.**

On the other hand, if you're one of the many people thinking: "I thought it was just me!" then I am here to tell you: it is not just you. We are everywhere.

The list of questions above encapsulates my own early career experience. I now hear these concepts echoed day in and day out, over and over, from those in my courses and workshops and those I work with as a strategy coach.

HOW DO I KNOW YOU'RE A STRATEGIST?

The profession of strategy is a funny one. Very few people decide: "I want to be a strategist when I grow up"; and aside from *Mad Men* it's not like there are many role models in the space. (And while *Mad Men* is an eerily accurate depiction of agency life—in any era—it's not exactly the model I want to perpetuate.) So let's talk for a minute about what being a strategist is *not*.

First, strategy *is not* being "smart." For too long, leaders and workplaces have conflated "strategic" and "smart." Thanks to Rob Estreitinho, the founder and head of strategy at Salmon Labs and one of my favorite sources on modern strategic thought, we now have this important clarification: "The job isn't to convince people that you're a smart person, it's to clarify situations so everyone can do the smart thing."

Second, having a strategist job title is not *being* a strategist. In my 30+ year career, I have held and hired for numerous roles with "strategist" in the name that were purely execu-

> **"The job isn't to convince people that you're a smart person, it's to clarify situations so everyone can do the smart thing."**

tional (and where strategic thinking was wholly unwelcome). So just having a "strategist" job title does not make you a strategist.

Being a strategist is completely separate from your job title or industry. You may be a strategist who works as a dishwasher, playing word games in your brain while you wash dishes. You may be a strategist who teaches elementary school, observing your students and adapting your teaching approaches based on the data you take in about each kid and how they learn. And yes, you may be a strategist who sits in a chair in an office with the title Chief Strategy Officer on the nameplate outside the door, for sure.

Here, I'm democratizing the role of strategist.

You are a strategist if you gather facts and observations about the world around you and use them to fuel insights. An insight is a truth that resonates with a person (or group of people), and sparks them to think differently or take some kind of action.

You may have come pre-programmed with a cognitive style that does this naturally. If you read books and research papers for fun and delight in spotting ways that wildly disparate information connects to create a new idea or approach, this might be you.

If you came pre-programmed with a strategist brain, that's only part of the puzzle. Now, you have to learn how to communicate those unique insights in ways that other people who are not wired the way you are can understand and engage with. To recruit others to your causes, you must somehow help them understand how you connected the dots (which can be harder than it sounds).

If you're thinking you did not come pre-programmed with a strategist brain, I hope this book provides a set of tools and practices to help you poke around inside yourself and meet and unblock your own inner strategist. Because if you think back to an earlier point in your life—before school and society conditioned it out of you—you probably had a chapter where you were curious and questioning like it was your job. That little you, asking "why?" so many times that your parent finally snapped back "because I said so!" and then slammed the door on the conversation is still inside of you. And that "little you" is who this book is for.

Any person can wield the tools coached here to enable their inner strategist to speak up for change with a higher likelihood of success when that's what's called for. The strategist in me recognizes the strategist in you.

Now that we agree that you are a strategist, this book is designed especially for you, to enable you to communicate the insights from your beautiful brain in ways others can rally behind. Because if you're going to change the world as only you can, the odds are low that you can do it all by yourself. You need a team.

The folks who relate to the five questions at the start of the introduction are traditionally critical behind-the-scenes players, playing a large role in the actual getting-stuff-done of many organizations. Someone has to dive into the details to do the research; make the plans; design the products; spot and predict which issues might turn into a crisis, and figure out how to mitigate them; and calmly and thoughtfully move through the crises that do happen, while running all the possible scenarios and making the best decisions they can with the information they have.

A lot of this work has been invisible. In fact, in the field of advertising, to say about a piece of creative that "the strategy is showing" means someone didn't do their job. "Good strategy" makes the work better, but you don't see the strategy itself.

The strategy is the scaffolding that the *stuff you ultimately see* rests on. The strategy is created, and *then* the visible work begins.

THE ROLE OF IDEAS

In the corporate environment, ideas often get all the glory. Big, shiny, new thinking can be the right tool for the job, especially when there are work challenges for which it makes sense to gather together and "ideate"—to develop and build out an idea through something like improv—a "yes, and" process of exploration and joint creation and collaboratively building alignment that is more imaginative than logical. The team creates and iterates together until they arrive at a finished product. The decisionmaker gives their feedback, changes are incorporated, and the work is produced and published.

But each idea is a gamble: you might win big, or you might lose big. Often the methods for evaluating and testing ideas are largely subjective: "Do I like this idea?" "Do you think this idea will work?" "What does the focus group say?" "Do we have the right focus group?" and on, and on. In a business environment where people and organizations are doing more with less, with the need to build nimble, adaptable organizations to keep up with a world changing faster than any of us can keep track of, having the best idea is not enough. It's hard to ignore the role that power and privilege play in the subjective assessment of ideas: when ideas are made the hero, opportunity, rewards, and recognition are still not equally accessible to everyone.

Increasingly, it's the folks who relate to the earlier five questions who are stepping out from the shadows and into the spotlight if anyone is to have any hope of solving the major organizational, cultural, and existential problems everyone faces. Today, insightful, curious, "linky" brains are an asset.

> **Today, leaders and individuals alike must be able to show their work.**

Today, leaders and individuals alike must be able to show their work—to strategize a path that establishes processes and goals to make those ideas a reality.

UNBLOCK YOUR INNER STRATEGIST

If you are a CEO responsible for delivering specific performance to a board or the market, you cannot afford the risk of making important decisions about your product, service, or business based on ideas alone. You, my friend, must do your homework. You must be able to trace your ideas back to data that is reasonable, logical, and can be understood by others.

If you are a business leader, you may sit six levels or more from the person implementing your business's core work. You need a way to facilitate collaboration and performance through communicating clear expectations, with enough context to enable people you may never even sit in the same room with to deliver on your vision without them having to be psychic.

If you are an implementer, you may be responsible for delivering empirically measurable results that have never been communicated to you as clear expectations. You can "wing it," doing your best to mind-read and follow the direction you're given by your leaders, or you can take the steering wheel and accept responsibility for your own measurable contributions to the organization's strategy.

If you are self-employed or pursuing a big vision of your own in any area of your life, you'll exhaust yourself by running with every idea that comes to mind; in entrepreneurial and visionary brains, ideas are like balls coming at you from a pitching machine without a regulator, flying at you so fast you can't even manage to swing at every one. You need some way to corral your big ideas and possibilities down to a workable direction, an aligned set of expectations, and a plan.

These are the skills you'll learn here.

You'll learn how to create your vision and identify objective metrics that indicate progress toward that vision. You will learn how to think big—how to develop insights based on strategic inputs, facts, and observations that pinpoint how you and your organization can do better.

Few, if any, strategists or strategic leaders come pre-programmed with these skills and competencies. Learning this straightforward toolkit—including a simple, usable Connected

You will learn how to think big.

Strategic One-Sheet and No-BS Objectives and Key Results—will get where you want to go.

If you aren't yet a leader in strategic development, the practices you'll learn here will arm you to operate more strategically; to make better choices so your time is focused on outcomes, not activity; and to ask and answer important questions enabling your team to align with your vision.

- What impacts or results are most important to achieve?
- Why do they matter?
- Why do they matter *now*?
- What might be possible to achieve?

- What could it mean to succeed wildly?
- How will you know, empirically, that you're making progress?
- What have you learned, or what are you learning?

You'll build your strategic skillset based on iteratively answering important questions like the above, which yield greater clarity, focus, alignment (and less unhealthy conflict and wasted time, energy, and frustration) for everyone involved.

That is how you unblock your inner strategist.

There's a reason this book is called *You Are a Strategist*, not "Are You a Strategist?"

In today's market and work world, every person can operate strategically—no matter how senior or tactical your role.

STRATEGY IS CLEAR EXPECTATIONS

Companies spend millions of dollars every year on in-house labor and consulting services on elegant, lengthy, smart strategy decks, only to have them promptly saved to a file-sharing site where they are rarely ever opened—until the company begins the process all over again in one, or three, or five years.

The company might then spend countless hours and dollars on project management systems and operational consulting in their efforts to become more "agile" and to increase their effectiveness. They might spend days in offsites and more dollars on HR consultants to learn how to improve their culture and impact, but somehow when they get back to the office the momentum evaporates and it's business as usual. Those well-intentioned project plans generate a lot of activity and output but may never yield the strategic outcomes the organization needs.

How do I know?

I spent the first act of my strategy career working for companies that fit that description (sometimes being part of the problem myself).

My colleagues and I were the ones crafting those compelling stories, building those beautiful decks, then working with our collaborators to deliver the work itself.

Almost every time, though, we were missing a critical piece of the puzzle: clear, objective alignment with the client on what success actually meant.

Sometimes that became apparent at the beginning. We'd gather for our kick-off and find out that the client's real world was significantly different than they'd told us during discovery. The work we'd pitched and won looked nothing like the work they expected us to do.

Sometimes we'd have a little honeymoon of alignment, then during implementation we'd become mired in round after round of review with increasingly unhappy and frustrated clients whose unspoken or unclear expectations were not being met.

Sometimes we'd get all the way through the creation to launching the work. We'd pat ourselves on the back for a job well done that would make a beautiful case study for our portfolio and win industry awards—and the client would let us know they were dissatisfied because the work didn't achieve the outcomes they imagined (but never clearly communicated).

My motivation and confidence dipped with each passing day whenever there wasn't an agreed, empirical measuring stick for our work together. The more this happened, the more I felt there had to be a better way.

Well, I was right. Over years of exploration, study, experimentation, and trial and error, I've developed that better way. And, as of 2024, it's worked with client organizations that have a combined annual economic impact of over $15 billion in revenue—along with an additional 300+ organizations implementing some elements of this approach based on my trainings and workshops and counting.

Over years of exploration, study, experimentation, and trial and error, I've developed that better way.

The better way explained in these pages—the Connected Strategic One-Sheet and No-BS OKRs process—enables changemakers like you to pave a clear path to impact. Unlike other approaches that can take weeks or months to implement, my workshop participants routinely complete the exercises in this book from start to finish over the course of four to six hours during a one- to two-week period.

That's right. In two weeks or less, you can lay the foundation for increased strategic impact—and career satisfaction and fulfillment while you're at it. You're about to become the strategist your organization and career has always needed.

Changemaker

1. An individual or entity that drives social and organizational transformation by actively pursuing innovation and actions that create positive and sustainable impact.

2. A person characterized by strategic vision, collaborative spirit, and an unwavering commitment to making a difference in their community or field of work.

3. A person who is a thinker *and* a doer, not afraid to challenge the status quo and inspire others to join their cause to create a better future.

These pages contain two big shifts that you need to know:

1. How to create a single-page connected strategy that distills your organizational strategy down to one usable page.
2. How to fill gaps in your strategic vision by implementing a coherent alignment layer to benefit your organization.

The first shift means creating a Connected Strategic One-Sheet, the tool I started using with clients to make their organizational strategy actually *useful* on a day-to-day basis. The second shift includes a specific, new approach to the widespread methodology known as Objectives and Key Results—the new approach I call No-BS OKRs.[1]

- **No-BS OKRs:** A straightforward, simple approach to creating and achieving objectives and key results (OKRs). No-BS OKRs have two parts: 1) clear, visionary, directional objectives, and 2) empirically[2] measurable key results—progress and outcome targets that align on what success means and reveal whether you're on or off track.

No-BS OKRs transform innovation-driven environments where performance hinges on improving human experiences, not just making numbers "look good."

---

[1] Some readers are turned off by the "vulgarity" of the term "No-BS," which I'll stand by the use of because no-BS is truly my goal. If you don't care for that term and wish to keep reading, you can mentally substitute "Evolutionary OKRs." I sometimes use that term in formal or more conservative settings where "No-BS" is frowned upon.

[2] Most OKR experts use the term "objectively" here (as in, "objectively measurable") to distinguish from goals that are assessed based on opinion. In the interests of not confusing the OKR element of objectives and "objectively measurable" in this context, I'm using "empirically." From here on in the book, when you see "empirically measurable" or "measurable" just know, what I'm saying there is that the item is based on data, facts, or quantified or countable observation, not opinions.

When you put into practice what you learn here, you'll clear the path for impact by yourself *and* your collaborators. You'll be able to:

- **Empower change.** Skip the chaos and dive straight into effective, impactful goal setting.
- **Boost innovation.** Foster a culture that values experimentation, creative solutions, and learning.
- **Quantify success.** Communicate expectations and measure impact far beyond the business metrics you're aware of today.

This book is your invitation into an innovative, rewarding, often misunderstood, and highly gate-kept area of business: the world of organizational strategy.

STRATEGY IS YOUR GOAL

If you're already a professional strategist, you may be scratching your head about why this book is so focused on goals when goal setting is not always part of a strategist's remit. The explanation is: motivation science.[3]

During my career as a creative agency strategist, every pitch I worked on started with goal setting. A lengthy discussion would then yield the same two goals: (1) win the work; and (2) do work that would get the client promoted.

---

[3] Motivation science is a cross-disciplinary field spanning "the science of motivation, including work carried out in all subfields of psychology, cognitive science, economics, sociology, management science, organizational science, neuroscience, and political science" (Society for the Study of Motivation, scienceofmotivation.org, www.scienceofmotivation.org/content.asp?contentid=138).

The problem was, even doing our very best work, our influence on those two goals was unbearably low. An agency can win the work in the room and lose it due to red tape in the procurement process; there are countless factors unrelated to our work that go into our client's performance evaluation. Those goals didn't give us clarity about what was important with this particular pitch or alignment on our purpose with this particular work.

I found myself in a deep, demotivated burnout. I loved my work, but the profound subjectivity was incompatible with my brain chemistry.

I started to wonder: What if we identified some other goals? What if we identified some selfish goals that mattered to us as professionals, that got us excited and motivated? So that even if we lost the work for some reason beyond our control, we still had a chance at satisfaction on our own self-motivated goal—over which we may have a bit more influence?

So I tried it.

Working in line with those early experimental self-set goals, I started to feel a strange new sense of confidence and self-esteem. My engagement with my work rebounded. My frustration diminished. And my collaboration with colleagues and leaders became less stressful and more clear.

At the time, I didn't know what was happening. I just knew that the more I focused on self-set, quantifiable goals, the happier I was at work.

Fast forward nearly a decade, and now—after years of specialty work in goal setting, operationalizing for goal attainment, and professional training in the art and science of human behavior change—it all makes sense.

Those early spontaneous experiments were consistent with decades of motivation science on goal setting and human behavior change.

Now, I know that those early spontaneous experiments were consistent with decades of motivation science on goal setting and human behavior change. And strategy achievement, at its core, is human behavior change.

Psychological research in the motivation sciences fields shows that human behavior change relies heavily on the creation of specific, actionable goals and a learning-focused approach. In this book, you're going to learn my methods for creating goals that increase learning, problem-solving, self-efficacy, intrinsic motivation, engagement, duration of goal pursuit, and other benefits that ultimately lead to higher performance.

I'm a firm believer in the power of the practices in this book not just to set goals but to transform the very mechanisms by which you'll achieve them, no matter your industry, your organization size, or your stage of career.

STRATEGY IS NONLINEAR, AND SO IS THIS BOOK

This book is divided into three parts, providing a fully-connected, complete toolkit for creating and achieving important strategic goals.

1. Strategic Direction
2. Strategic Alignment
3. Strategy Achievement

Part 1 is about establishing direction. Having clear vision and direction to follow is important both to increase your chances of success and, also, to enable you to bring others along on the journey with you effectively.

Part 2—and this is where objectives and key results come in—shows that to achieve maximum on your strategic vision, you need visibility into the facts of your progress and achievement. You need a solid dashboard; not one that "looks good," but one based on facts and honesty since you can only do better if you have data on where you are right now. Objectives and key results (OKRs) and the other practices in this part fill in gaps in your current planning model with critical tactics about your progress, successes, and failures.

Finally, in Part 3, you'll find a resource guide with wide-ranging topics to architect the behavior and operating changes necessary to achieve your strategy. This section is "choose your own adventure," since each reader will be in a different environment and stage. Read what applies to you, skip what doesn't, and come back to it as a reference as your career evolves.

I've made every effort to create a book here designed to be useful for linear and non-linear thinkers alike. This book can be read start to finish, each chapter building on the previous. But you can also pick and choose which sections are of interest to you and skip any sections that don't apply for now and come back to them later.

Once you've finished working your way through this book, you'll have had the opportunity to practice with the frameworks and practices I use working with enterprises from the Fortune 100 to solopreneurs. These tools allow organizations to increase impact, to stop wasting valuable human labor, and to achieve higher rates of human engagement—employee engagement or your own personal career satisfaction and engagement. These same practices can indeed be applied personally, so you can envision and build the life you want to lead.

While you're at it, you'll learn (by doing) a number of important practices, skills, and mindset shifts that will make the most of that big, beautiful brain of yours—your curiosity, creativity, intrinsic motivation, and experimentation—not to mention confidence-building step-by-step exercises and practices that reduce the cognitive overhead of creating strategic deliverables. It's all fuel for your strategic brain.

Speaking of exercises . . .

If you are a worksheet person, this book has a companion: *The No-BS OKRs Workbook*. The workbook includes quick versions of basic No-BS OKRs words and meanings and fourteen worksheets, with expanded instructions for the exercises mentioned in this book. *The No-BS OKRs Workbook* is available both as a downloadable PDF or as a print book. The downloadable PDF version is available at findrc. co/pdfworkbook, and the print book information is at youareastrategist.com.

TL^DR: STRATEGIST TAKEAWAYS

This book explains:

- How to distill your strategy down to a single page to hold yourself to achieving what's most important.
- How No-BS OKRs—the specific implementation approach I created and work with—can improve your leadership and career effectiveness.
- How to create clear, focused, aligned OKRs for your team and yourself.
- Advanced skills for the big thinker.

By learning the above skills, you'll become better acquainted with your own inner strategist and be ready to lead (from the back or any other chair in the office) in today's ever-changing business world. If you follow the pattern my clients do, you'll do so while increasing employee engagement, your own career impact, and your own career fulfillment.

"What if I have a hard time even getting motivated?"

Not everyone picking up this book is going to feel excited or motivated about yet another deep dive into performance enhancement—and that's okay. If you are burned out; if you're in an environment that isn't bringing out the best in you; if you've had bad experiences that make you feel jaded about investing time and energy to try again—you're 100% welcome here. This is not a place for toxic positivity, toxic productivity, or performative goal setting.

You are here to create anti-perfect goals and to treat your goals and goal-pursuit efforts with unconditional positive regard and self-compassion.

Begin to notice every step you take toward goal setting and achievement as progress. Reading this chapter gets you further along on your progress than doing nothing. Even thinking about your goals is progress.

It is 100% okay (and can be effective) to create OKRs that reflect exactly where you are. Your goals may be more focused on pain relief, self-care, or trying to rekindle your own joy, not focused on performance or big outcomes. That's great! Build your own foundation of well-being, engage with your life, and very selfishly prioritize what you can to reconnect and rekindle your intrinsic motivation. Your future performance depends on you moving successfully through the slump and coming out the other side rested, recharged, and excited for whatever comes next.

STRATEGIC DIRECTION

In motorsports, there is a fundamental truth: You must have *direction* before you go to full throttle.

What that means is, if you're in a turn where you can't yet see your exit (the point at which the road before you straightens out so you can see confidently what's ahead), you don't yet have direction. If you go to full throttle without direction, the odds are high you will have a sudden and painful date with the asphalt beneath you.

Instead, skilled riders are patient through turns and know not to apply full throttle until they can see the way forward clearly. At that point—when they have direction—they can hit the gas without falling down.

Slow is smooth, and smooth is fast.

It's the same in business. If you kick off your effort with enthusiasm and full force and get to work, it's possible you will succeed without a crash. But you can reduce the risk of falling down by taking a moment to be patient and develop your vision of what's ahead.

In this part, you'll find your direction and position yourself to apply maximum throttle with less likelihood of an unpleasant outcome.

- Begin by looking at some common-sense and straightforward ways to ensure that you have a clear vision of what you're aiming toward in **Chapter 1: "Making Strategy Usable and Useful."**

- Then, calibrate on the performance potential of the environment you work in with **Chapter 2: "What's Possible: The No-BS High-Performance Readiness Model."**

- Finally, complete the vision exercise in **Chapter 3: "The Big Think"** to focus your goal setting and make creation of high-quality OKRs faster and easier.

1

MAKING STRATEGY USABLE AND USEFUL

Ninety percent of my time is spent working with clients to craft objectives and key results (OKRs), which we'll get to in Part 2. But the most enthusiastic fan mail I receive by far comes in about the practices you'll become familiar here with in Part 1.

This chapter begins with an important reconciliation step, showing how the pieces of a Connected Strategic Stack fit together within organizations. Then, it explains a new practice for sense-making in even the most complicated and fast-moving organization: the Connected Strategic One-Sheet. Finally, you'll assess and calibrate on your organization's change readiness using the No-BS High-Performance Readiness Model.

The Connected Strategic Stack is an abstraction of an organization's full strategy-to-implementation framework. The Connected Strategic One-Sheet is a distillation of an organization's most important strategic elements to a single page. The No-BS OKRs High-Performance Readiness Model diagnoses where in the journey a specific organization is.

HOW DOES STRATEGY CONNECT TO IMPLEMENTATION?

You're certainly aware of Shiny New Thing Syndrome; it's when methodologies and practices are introduced as magical-thinking answers to all that ails an organization. What you'll learn here is not that. In reality, methodologies and practices must be coherently reconciled with the organization's existing operations and behavior to be of any use.

Shiny New Thing Syndrome: When methodologies and practices are introduced as magical-thinking answers to all that ails an organization.

Nearly every organization has some form of strategic plan—articulating the organization's vision, purpose, and reason for being—and some sort of delivery plans—the identification of initiatives, projects, and work that the organization intends to complete. In many organizations, that is the strategic implementation stack. There's a slide deck somewhere on a file share that talks about the big picture stuff and a bunch of projects and tasks in one or more project management systems—and never the twain shall meet.

So most organizations lack connective tissue between their strategic artifacts and the delivery layer, which can lead to a free-for-all of activities. The strategy is often created by senior executives (or their consulting agency) and tells a beautiful, aspirational story about the vision the organization wishes to bring to life. Then each person or team plans the workloads they believe are most important. If you're lucky, some workloads may be closely aligned to the organization's strategy; often, teams may be hard at work on pet projects or efforts that are "how we've always done it," which bear little relevance to the organization's strategy. Without connective tissue to tie the strategy to implementation, team members may be wasting time and resources on workloads that don't contribute to the organization's strategic achievement.

How Many Organizations Strategize and Plan

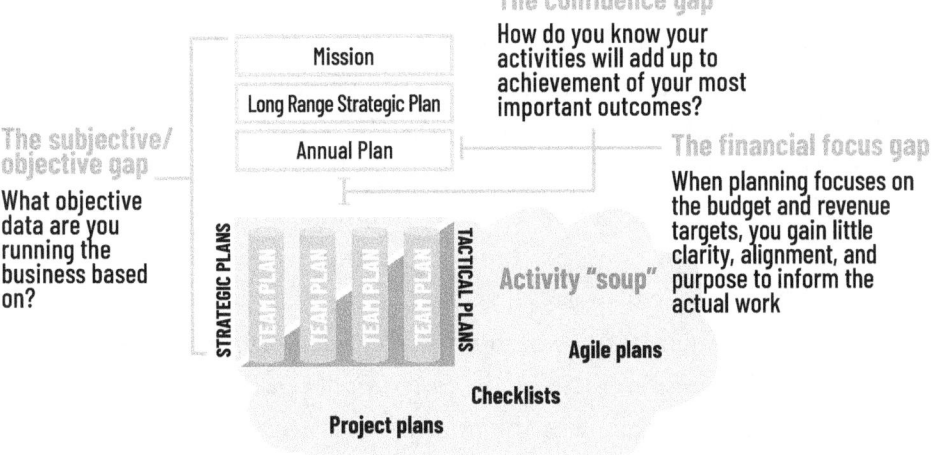

This typical approach creates three big gaps that can be problematic for the organization.

First, the confidence gap. Executives are responsible for projecting optimism and confidence to shareholders and board members and for achieving aggressive growth goals. Most leaders have an abundance of optimism, hope, and trust in their teams. But many organizations operate without data to know—empirically—if their organization is on track. Too many leaders "perform" confidence based on subjective information about how their business is operating. Has a manager ever asked you to "make the numbers look good" at a leadership meeting or to spin bad news to make it sound not so bad? That's subjectivity at work. An environment where the executive's subjective confidence needs to be maintained is one where people are not always free to speak up when something is wrong or at risk—the performance of confidence must be maintained. But the CEOs I work with crave objective, or empirical, data on how their business is performing; that way, whether the numbers are good or bad, they know the truth, and can lead with confidence based on actual data.

Next is the financial focus gap. In the typical approach described above, the goals specified in that high-level strategy are almost always heavily focused on financial measures. That gives sales and senior executives clarity, but when success is only measured in terms of revenue or profitability, non-sales and non-finance employees are left wondering, "How does this apply to me and my work?"

Finally, the typical approach leaves organizations with a big expectation gap. Organizations aren't always precise with expectations when explaining strategic goals. Some goals may be mandatory, with serious consequences for non-achievement. Other goals are aspirational. Sometimes, companies need to grow or innovate, which requires safety to experiment—and to even fail—in the pursuit of progress. Your company's aspirational goals are an experiment in how your organization might do better—they represent something to strive for. But blending mandatory and aspirational goals without clear distinctions causes a few challenges.

- Employees may set easy goals they know they can achieve, which leaves potential performance on the table.
- Employees may overcommit to aspirational goals, treating them as mandatory, which presents the risk of burnout.
- Trust erodes when people experience negative consequences for not achieving an aspirational goal.

So what is your new secret weapon for closing these performance-zapping gaps?

The Connected Strategic Stack. This simple framework connects high-level strategy with day-to-day implementation by adding an alignment layer that fills in all three gaps.

THE CONNECTED STRATEGIC STACK

I developed the idea of the Connected Strategic Stack after realizing my clients needed a simple way to: understand the missing pieces of their existing strategic implementation; align on how to fill the gaps mentioned above; and determine whether they already had something in their stack doing the job of objectives (aspirational, directional goals communicating a sense of shared purpose) and key results (empirically measurable goals clarifying what success and progress mean in a quantifiable way.

While not all organizations include every item in this model, most do benefit from externalizing as much of their strategic stack as possible and assessing where they may have gaps.

A Connected Strategic Stack might include elements as seen on the chart on the left.

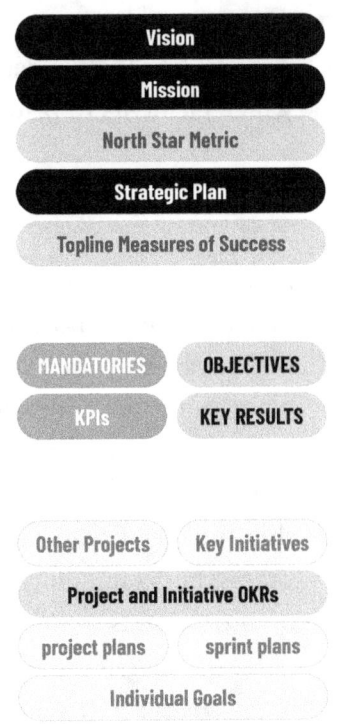

Connected Strategic Stack

Vision

Mission

North Star Metric

Strategic Plan

Topline Measures of Success

MANDATORIES | OBJECTIVES

KPIs | KEY RESULTS

Other Projects | Key Initiatives

Project and Initiative OKRs

project plans | sprint plans

Individual Goals

As you can see:

- Organization-wide shared strategic artifacts sit at the top, in the first five rows.
- The alignment layer (the next two rows, including OKRs) derive from the strategic artifacts.
- The initiatives and activity plans (rows eight through ten) are designed to maximize achievement on upline OKRs (and other critical business-as-usual or run-the-business functions).
- Finally, individual goals (and growth and development plans, line eleven) are created with alignment to all the above.

Now, let's look in detail at each layer of the stack so you can assess which elements to prioritize for your organization.

Strategic artifacts

At the top of an ideal Connected Strategic Stack are strategic artifacts, in the form of a long-term vision or mission; a North Star metric; a three- to five-year strategic plan or an annual operating plan; and topline measures.

These artifacts are typically spread across several documents and sometimes housed in file servers specific to certain levels of leadership (not the organization at large). The items in this layer shape a shared understanding of why the organization exists and what the organization is trying to do.

- **Vision:** A forward-looking statement that describes the changed future an organization aspires to create. The vision enunciates the organization's reason for being in terms of its essential purpose. A vision acts as a cornerstone or guiding beacon to inspire employees, inform decision-making, align stakeholders, and tell customers why the organization exists.

- **Mission:** A statement that describes the activity of an organization in the context of the organization's vision. An organization's mission statement further assists customers in understanding what to expect in terms of what the organization does in the world.

- **North Star metric:** A single metric that describes the organization's reason for being in a quantifiable way, answering the question: "What is the single most important impact measure we aspire to achieve?" The most effective North Star metrics are non-financial, describing the most important metric due to which, when that metric is healthy, revenue follows. Often this means the North Star metric is a usage, customer experience, or other product or customer metric.

- **Topline metrics:** The three to five key metrics that drive the organization's success. Topline metrics are the critical health measures. When they are healthy, the organization is moving in the right direction. When they are not, the organization is at risk. One (or maximum two) topline metrics may be financial metrics, but like the North Star metric, choosing non-financial topline metrics provides the organization important clarity about where performance should be focused to maximize revenue realization.

A North Star metric is not present in all organizations, but when it is, it can provide essential information to inform subsequent OKRs. The term "North Star metric" has been used in a variety of ways by different authors. For the type of human-impact organizations I primarily work with, the North Star metric is defined as the most important non-financial measure of the organization's success or impact. In other words, when that metric is healthy and growing, leadership knows the organization is as well.

Every organization's strategic plan, if they have one, is going to look different. Some are truly strategic, providing clarity both about where the organization is heading (and why) and some of the critical measures of success the organization is aiming for. One business I work with, for example, has a ten-year strategic plan for which they are in Year 6. At least annually, they check in on their progress. They adjust their strategic plan if necessary due to changes in market conditions or operating environment. (Most businesses, for example, in 2024 are revisiting their strategic plans in the face of rapid large language models and generative AI development.) They then rely on the refined strategic plan to inform the rest of their planning activities for the year.

> **Every organization's strategic plan, if they have one, is going to look different**

When organizations operate without a document like the above, it's often because their field is changing so rapidly that they don't feel it worthwhile to forecast years ahead. (Think about those LLM and generative AI organizations that are literally creating the future as I type.) These organizations substitute an annual operating plan or a budget for a strategic plan.

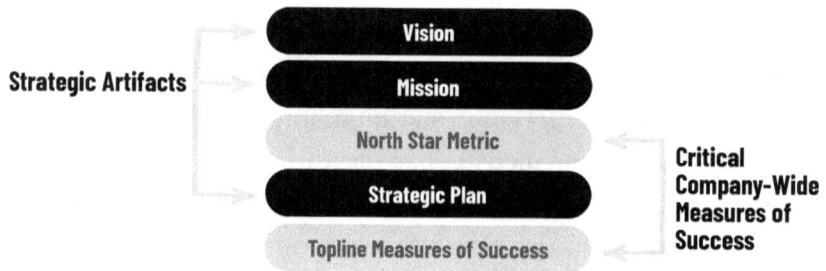

Topline measures are the small number of most important metrics that show progress toward upline strategic goals. When your toplines and your North Star metric are healthy and growing, you know your organization is also. One of your topline measures may be a financial or revenue health metric, but resist the common tendency to make your North Star and topline measures all financial. These are important measures of progress and success for an entity, no doubt; however, they do little to help people make aligned, cooperative decisions informed by the desire to work together to achieve those goals.

Metrics like customer and employee satisfaction, business health indicators like customer retention or loyalty, customer lifetime value, and any number of industry or company-specific critical benchmarks make for strong topline measures. In my own business, we don't have a revenue topline. We focus on customer satisfaction, team satisfaction, and our North Star measure—the number of people that this work benefits—rather than pursuing a specific revenue target. When our chosen indicators are headed in the right direction, the revenue follows. Focusing on meaningful toplines yields experiences for our client humans that greatly exceed the experiences we'd provide if we were focusing specifically on revenue maximization.

When I start a consulting project, not all of the elements at the top of the stack may be accounted for, but almost every organization I work with ultimately identifies these strategic inputs by the end of our engagement. The North Star metric and topline measures give the organization valuable direction about what matters most for the organization's success and can assist teams to set goals designed for maximum progress. Otherwise, team members might try to craft key results based on guessing how the organization will ultimately quantify success.

The alignment layer

The alignment layer (see details and illustration below) in the Connected Strategic Stack sits between strategy and delivery. It ensures that the guiding navigation has signal for operational progress and risks so everyone is clear about the organization's most important criteria for success. The alignment layer contains objectives and key results, as well as important key performance indicators (KPIs). Key results metrics prioritize improvement toward a specific target; KPI metrics ensure the day-to-day business is staying healthy. The alignment layer also identifies any mandatory goals that must be met at 100% completion or there may be consequences. In short, the alignment layer defines how in the near-term the organization quantifies organizational health, progress, and success.

> **An alignment layer that is coherent with topline strategic inputs is missing in most organizations.**

An alignment layer that is coherent with topline strategic inputs is missing in most organizations. Very few organizations—even among those "doing OKRs"—have identified actual key results (empirically quantifiable measures of progress and success, with a clear start and finish value). Some organizations have extensive dashboards chock full of metrics (with little actual insight resulting from all that math); others adopt KPIs based on what's easy or available to measure and not always what's most important.[4] The whole reason for developing key results, however, is to quantify what's most important (even if it's not possible to measure perfectly today) and to identify the clear target for each.

Another big issue with the alignment layer, when an organization has one, involves imprecision in words and meanings. The No-BS OKRs methodology depends on the use of well-defined words with

---

[4]   Chapter 8: "Deep Dive into No-BS Key Results" will look at tactics for creating key results around what's most important, not only what's easy to measure today.

consistent meanings to create an alignment layer that connects what you do to your strategy and purpose. For example, organizations seldom have clarity about which goals are mandatory and which are stretch goals. Mandatory goals must be achieved 100%, and they are not safe to fail on. Stretch goals—the type most commonly represented in key results—move people into speculative or uncertain territory. Therefore, it must be safe to try (and even fail) in the pursuit of progress.

And, it's critical to know which is which. Many organizations confuse or conflate the two. They call their alignment layer "stretch goals," but then mete out consequences if the goals are not achieved by an arbitrary amount of "enoughness" (which is typically not communicated in advance). Consequences for lack of "enough" achievement on a stretch goal is one of the largest sources of aversion to OKRs.

> **Be crisp about words and meanings.**

To avoid this incoherence and lack of shared understanding, be sure to adopt a clear, well-defined set of terms to guide your organization toward greater alignment. In your alignment layer, be crisp about words and meanings.

- **Mandatory goals** are 100% must-achieve targets for which your team is not safe to fail. There may be consequences for non-achievement; therefore, the organization must prioritize and support mandatory goals with the required budget and resources.

- **Key performance indicators (KPIs)** are the constantly tracked business metrics subsidiary to mandatory goals that indicate whether the organization is in alignment, healthy, and headed in the right direction.
- **Objectives** are aspirational, inspired, directional statements of intent that describe what's most important and why it matters for the goal term.
- **Key results** are empirically measurable stretch goals that align to objectives and describe how the organization is currently quantifying progress or success for the sake of achieving its most important outcomes (and learning and improving for the future).

A note on KPIs: If an organization had a human body, KPIs would be its blood pressure, pulse, and cholesterol levels—the metrics you keep an eye on to make sure the body stays healthy. KPIs vary widely by organization, industry, and discipline. Every platform, piece of software, and dashboard is chock full of potential things to measure; your KPIs are the subset that you monitor closely because they signal which way your business is heading. You can think of them as mini topline measures, or you can think of topline measures as uber KPIs. The two are related, but your toplines should be only the handful of most important metrics. KPIs make up the larger set of metrics across your business that you keep an eye on.

> **In the No-BS OKRs model, OKRs are aspirational stretch goals**

In the No-BS OKRs model, OKRs are aspirational stretch goals for which your mandatory goals and KPIs can provide clarity on performance in your knowable territories. But, if you are reading this book, odds are your work is already taking you into the unknown, into uncharted territory. It may not be realistic to set or forecast goals with precision in this new space, so mandatory goals may need to be set very conservatively.

No-BS OKRs let you align on goals that describe the changed future that you're trying to achieve. They're like a forecast of what you might be able to achieve if everything goes right. OKRs are treated differently than mandatory goals because with the mandatories the goal is attainment (if they aren't attained, there be dragons). With OKRs, the goal is high performance but also learning, experimentation, and progress.

We'll talk more about mandatory goals in the key results chapter. I show them separately in the Connected Strategic Stack for clarity, but many organizations include mandatory goals in their key result lists. This can work if they are clearly labeled as such. For now it's enough to say that in the No-BS OKRs model, your key results are presumed to be stretch measures for which you are safe to try and even fail in the pursuit of progress and learning *unless* they are clearly labeled as mandatory goals.

> **In No-BS OKRs, key results are stretch measures for which you are safe fail.**

The implementation layer

While most organizations have an implementation layer already, often that layer may lack strategic alignment. Also, many organizations are driven by their implementation layer. They decide first what they plan to do or what their most important initiatives are and then discuss what results those activities or plans may yield—and that's the extent of their strategic implementation alignment. No-BS OKRs make it clear that to be effective, you need more.

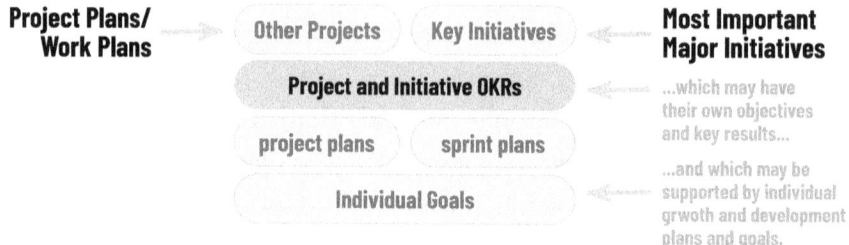

In a full Connected Strategic Stack, an organization identifies the following items in the implementation layer:

- **Initiatives** are the major workloads requiring broad or cross-functional awareness of status and risk that contribute to the achievement of the organization's strategic priorities.

- Teams and people may identify **other projects** that support strategic priorities and business-as-usual workloads.

- Specific **project/initiative OKRs** are developed so that the working team has clarity on what progress and success means for that workload (and to ensure alignment with the upline strategic goals).

- Activity is then designed in the form of **project plans** or **sprint plans**.

- **Individual goals** can then be drafted by each person in the organization to orient themselves toward aligned clarity about what's expected of them and to create plans and goals that allow them to maximally contribute to the organization's priorities.[5]

---

[5]   There are some important science-based best practices around incentivizing individual performance that most organizations ignore completely. I don't address individual goal setting in exhaustive detail in this book; for more information about creating an aligned individual goal model (and rewards and incentives system) that does not create disincentives for setting aspirational, inspirational, stretch goals, visit findrc.co/perf_mgmt.

A COMPLETE CONNECTED STRATEGIC STACK

Connected Strategic Stack

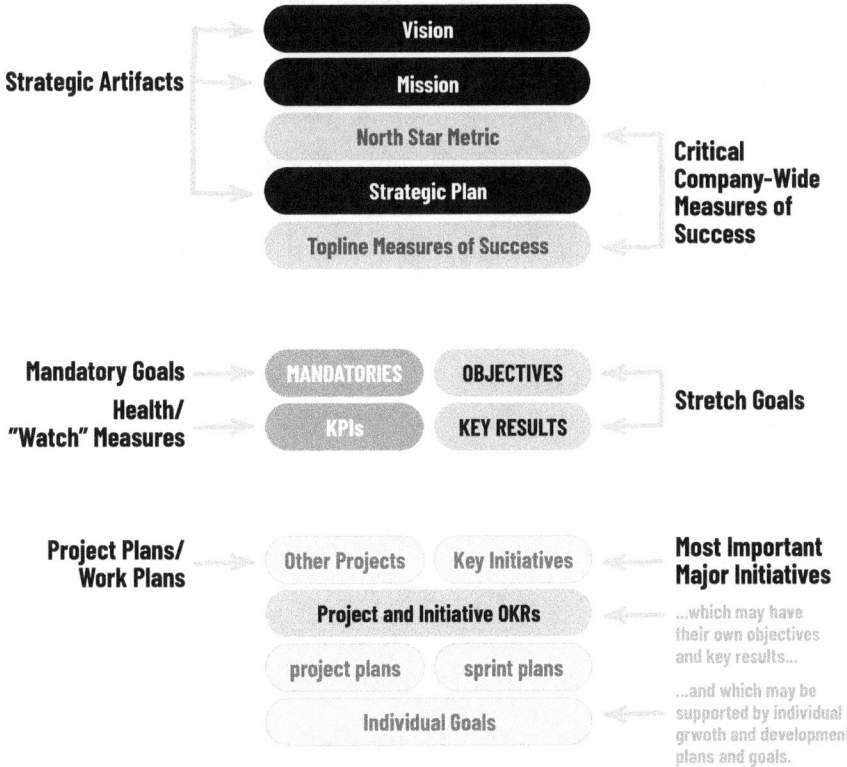

Not every organization is going to complete every element of the Connected Strategic Stack—and that's okay! An organization does not need to have every one of these individual boxes present in their approach to strategic implantation to be successful. In smaller organizations and those in a rapid-change environment, there may naturally be fewer and lighter durable strategic inputs. Some organizations may use annual company-level OKRs as their "strategy," much to the dismay of business strategists, planners, and OKR experts, but I still say that the clarity they give their organization by adopting annual company-level OKRs is much better than nothing.

Your organization's stack may look different than this one. But if you're considering "hiring" OKRs to do the job of increasing focus, clarity, and alignment, they'll be better at that job if you allow strategic inputs to narrow their focus so they're not an arbitrary list of directions and measures. If the bulk of your focus has been on quantifying what you're doing instead of what outcomes will create the transformation your organization needs, then the stack can reveal the gaps that may be impeding your progress.

Questions to reflect on for your own strategic stack:

- Which elements exist today (or are easy to decipher from existing artifacts)?
- Which elements should be the priority to define consistently, to increase shared meaning and understanding?
- Which elements should be included to increase your organization's strategic alignment and impact?

CONNECTED STRATEGIC ONE-SHEET

I don't remember the first time I created the Connected Strategic One-Sheet, but since then, this approach to developing a strategic input has been a head-turning feature of every sales cycle I've pitched and every executive review I've delivered.

Here's an example of the simple One-Sheet format I use with each element filled in for a hypothetical educational products company:

EduToy Co Strategic Inputs on a Page

Vision	Mission
For every child to have the chance to love learning	Build infrastructure to scaffold early-childhood education globally

North Star Measure

Number of children served through Loving Learning Initiatives

Topline Measures

Innovation	Growth	Sustainability	Customer Sat
Number of new product releases	Number of new countries served	Environmental Impact Index	Global Learning-is-Fun Rating

Objectives

Innovation + Growth	Experiences + Customer	Sustainability	Financial Health
Continuously innovate to inspire a love of learning	Invest to create memorable brand experiences in-store and online infused with the benefits of "fun"	Reduce our environmental impact to contribute to a sustainable future	Improve operational efficiency now to establish a foundation as a high-impact brand building a legacy

The One-Sheet is the next logical step after the Connected Strategic Stack; it consolidates the information needed to develop high-quality OKRs from the various decks and docs and dashboards to provide one single page of direction for the upcoming goal cycle.

The purpose of this single-page view is to keep people from having to dig through piles of documents and slides to understand what's relevant when creating OKRs.

When is a One-Sheet essential?

A One-Sheet distillation of your most important strategic inputs is important for any company to have. A well-written strategic plan has an executive summary. Why shouldn't all organizations also have a simple, no-fuss, single-page executive summary providing an at-a-glance distillation of strategic artifacts? This format is among the most powerful (and simple/no-fuss to create) I've seen yet.

A One-Sheet is important if you aspire to have multiple aligned layers of goals, providing detail for various levels of the organization and working group. (I'll dive into this in much more detail in Chapter 11: "OKRs at Scale.")

When there are company-level OKRs (referred to as "Level 1" OKRs) at the C-level of an organization, for example, those OKRs may provide all of the clarity for the CEO's direct reports to localize OKRs to their various functional organizations ("Level 2" OKRs).

But something funky happens when you travel any deeper into the organization. At the next level of localization ("Level 3" OKRs, or team or initiative OKRs for cross-functional projects), this can become counterintuitive. Just like with a game of telephone, decisions are made at each step of localization that may be inaccurately translated. Because you're getting closer to implementation, it may be necessary to "zoom out" to the One-Sheet for a reminder of what's most important from a big-picture standpoint. When a team looks at their own Level 2 OKRs and the company's Level 1 OKRs and struggles to see how their work connects in, they can refer to the One-Sheet for direction and inspiration. Between the vision and mission statements and the metrics in the North Star and topline metrics, anyone in

Why shouldn't all organizations have a simple, single-page executive summary providing an at-a-glance distillation of strategic artifacts?

the organization should be able to spot something to hang their own OKRs on.

In most settings, the One-Sheet follows the Connected Strategic Stack closely down to the level of topline measures, themes, and objectives. I often find a sweet spot at the level of themes and objectives; that gives the organization clarity about the "uber KPIs" the organization is using to quantify its health (in its topline measures) and what the themes are for the upcoming goal cycle (and objectives if they exist).

I have also worked with organizations that have decided not to create OKRs at the top level for various reasons that make sense for their business (e.g., extremely rapid rates of change; extreme uncertainty in the near-term forecast; extreme volatility that may mean large reorganizations or course changes). These companies create One-Sheets as an interim strategic input for Level 2 and below OKR creation and individual goal setting. If a leadership team is not yet comfortable with creating and leading with OKRs but their organization is enthusiastically experimenting with them, this can be a win-win for the organization; it brings clarity of direction from the top for teams and people to align to, and the bottoms-up OKRs may allow skeptical leaders to see the benefits of OKRs before adopting them at the top level.

The first time you attempt a Connected Strategic One-Sheet may require a bit of digging, but you may be surprised how intuitive it can be to create with the organizational knowledge you already have in your head, even without doing formal discovery and analysis.

EXERCISE: LAYING THE GROUNDWORK TO CREATE YOUR ONE-SHEET

Step 1: Gather your strategic inputs

Reminding yourself of your organization's strategic inputs brings focus to creating OKRs aligned to the strategies. The first step therefore in developing OKRs is drawing together your strategic inputs.

Few organizations already have an effective One-Sheet as an input to OKR creation. Most organizations have strategic insight spread across many documents—if it's written down at all. At the company level, examples of documents that may be considered strategic inputs include:

- A business plan, which generally includes the organization's mission, vision, and reason for being.
- An annual operating plan or budget documents.
- A company/corporate strategic plan.
- Upline OKRs (e.g., company-level OKRs, as opposed to goals deeper in the organization).
- Any number of other documents with the word "plan" or "strategy" in them, including financial plans, marketing plans, sales plans, corporate social responsibility or sustainability plans, and risk management or crisis plans that sit at the company or enterprise level.

If you're working on goal creation as a solopreneur, startup founder, or small business owner, you may have strategic inputs like the above. Or, you may have few (or no) inputs to your goal-drafting process—and that's okay. This chapter will get you started.

If you're working on goal creation in an individual context as an employee, you may find strategic inputs in the form of:

- The types of documents listed above.
- Departmental plans.
- Project briefs.
- Your job description.
- Your most recent performance evaluation.

Whatever role you're in, even if you have none of the above, you can follow the instructions in this chapter to create your own draft One-Sheet.

In the workshops I teach, creating One-Sheets is consistently an exercise participants find valuable. We do this step before we begin thinking about objectives or key results. You're encouraged to do so right now if having a simple, one-page input to your OKR creation will help you identify and understand what's most important.

But I understand you're probably in a hurry. If getting right into OKR creation is more important for you, you can skip ahead to this book's Part 2.

Step 2: Review the documents

Review all the strategic input documents you gathered in Step 1.

- Capture any language you see that communicates the organization's reason for being.
  - **Highlight or underline** any language that might inform an objective.
  - **Circle or box** any words you recognize as potentially interesting metrics or measures.
  - Also circle or box any directional words, like "increase," "decrease," "reduce," "improve," since they signal potential measurement opportunity or measurability.

Step 3: Assemble your One-Sheet

Company Name One-Sheet

Vision	Mission
The change the organization exists to make in the world; your reason for being.	The organization's role in achieving that change.

North Star Measure

The organization's most important non-financial success metric. When this number is healthy, the organization is healthy and growing.

Topline Measures

Additional topline most important success metrics: the KPIs or health metrics you watch to determine whether of not you're maximizing progress toward the vision, mission, and North Star.

Objectives

In what direction(s) do you need improvement to make progress in the near-term (this quarter/this year)?

Give yourself a big box with the headers as shown in the example, and drop anything potentially useful from Step 2 into the One-Sheet.

My favorite way to conduct this exercise in my live workshops is with a large piece of paper or a whiteboard and sticky notes (or a canvas app like Miro, Mural, or Microsoft Whiteboard). You want to be able to move things around easily until you're happy with how your inputs are organized and so you can think and create nonlinearly. Of course, you can also take notes in pencil on a sheet of paper and erase and edit as you go or revise in iterative versions.

Step 4: Pull it all together

Now, take a look at the yield of your work.

1. The top-level buckets you drew boxes or circles around can be consolidated down to a manageable number (usually not more than four or five) and each be placed into the theme slot.

2. The highlighted or underlined concepts can be grouped together in some logical way that gives you an idea about what bucket or theme those concepts may align to. Add that in one of the theme spots and then drop the conceptual language into the box for that theme.

3. Or, is your situation simpler than that? You could just drop your highlighted concepts into an empty objectives box (and skip the theme box for now, or maybe forever). The directional or conceptual language you highlighted can be assembled in the objectives area of the template.

4. Review each piece of potential language and consider: "Does this align to a theme identified above?" If so, drop it there.

Themes, territories, groups, buckets, and categories

One of the tools in a strategist's (or designer's) toolkit is a card sort. I became aware of card sorts in the context of human-centered design, where individual pieces of information are placed on cards (index cards, sticky notes) so that they can be arranged into categories. Card sorting is a method for collaboratively thinking: information gets externalized onto cards that each person can see; then the group can discuss and align on whether or how each piece of information relates with the others. It's a practice for organizing information in a way that helps different people align on a theory about a shared mental model.

A huge part of OKR creation is externalizing thinking to achieve a shared, aligned, mental model, so the card sort is a helpful practice to remember.

In creating OKRs, you can use a version of this practice to group your thoughts together to identify your objective "themes." We'll also talk about key result and possibly initiative "territories." If those terms are confusing, you can think of them as groups, categories, or the term that I hear every week in my work with clients and students. When I introduce the concept of objective themes, or key result territories, someone says: "You mean, like buckets?" and I say "Yes, exactly." So don't let the word "theme" or "territory" trip you up—you can think of them as "groups" or "buckets" if that's more intuitive for you.

Any potential measurements you circled may be a topline measure, a key result, or a KPI, but it's not time to dive into that level of detail just yet. For now, just divide the potential measurement indicators into two categories.

1. Might the measure be a topline measure? Topline measures, remember, are the most important contributors to organizational success (and you should typically only have four or five of them, total). If you spot any potential topline measures, add them to the topline box on your worksheet.

2. Is the measure not topline but still potentially important enough to be a KPI or to be the basis of a key result? If so, drop it into a parking lot for further consideration when you get to creating key results.

Step 5: Final touches

When you're done pulling your notes into your worksheet, sit back and look at your One-Sheet.

- Is anything missing that you can fill in based on what you know, personally?
- Is anything missing that you feel you can't complete OKR creation without? If so, identify who can help you fill that gap, and then get it filled.
- Are there gaps where there isn't any information because clarity doesn't exist yet? If so, can you fill that gap with a quick theory, experiment, or draft? If that's not possible, just leave it blank for now. (But usually, a theory, experiment, or draft is better than a blank when you get to the next step, so don't let "perfect" be the enemy of "good enough." If you can jot a quick gap-filler without overthinking it, do it.)

Once you've completed your draft One-Sheet, take a minute to review it with your supervisor, colleagues, or important collaborators to get feedback on whether your view of the stack is aligned. Doing that alignment check early at this low-fidelity draft point ensures that the OKRs you create next are quality-in, quality-out (instead of the dreaded garbage-in, garbage-out).

The power of intentional fidelity

Does the idea of sharing your quickly-drafted, low-fidelity, very rough One-Sheet with others make your heart pound with anxiety? Is your instinct to take a few hours to spiff it up and maybe put it into a slide before anyone else sees it?

If so, that means that you're probably a diligent, thoughtful worker to whom it's important to put your best work forward, i.e., not presenting until you've crafted a high-fidelity version. It may also mean that you've experienced conditioning that has resulted in some perfectionism.

I see a lot of clients who self-identify as overthinkers, over-workers, over-preparers, or perfectionists. If they don't self-identify, they do voice an audible sigh of relief to be "seen" when I ask them if they struggle with those behaviors after I hear their stories.

The cool thing about any default mode is that there is always a non-default mode that can be intentionally learned, practiced, and used strategically. The instinct telling you to do more work on your One-Sheet before sharing it with anyone reflects your default mode. The non-default option is to consider sharing your One-Sheet *exactly how it is right now*. It may be messy and rough and unrefined and not at all pretty or ready for prime time. That's what makes now the time to share it.

Have you gotten your rough thinking down on the page? If so, what makes sense as a next step?

A. To invest time and energy into making it "pretty" and more refined.

B. To invest time and energy into ensuring it's aligned and correct before you spend cycles on refinement.

Often, instincts say "A" because the assumption is that people will respond more favorably to more finished work. But in a lot of cases— especially if you're strategically wired—it can be beneficial to take the non-default option of "B." How do you know which to choose?

• Is the work more in your singular domain, fairly final, and you're ready for critical feedback? Then the "A" door may make sense.

- Is the work something you're going to be collaborating on to complete? Will other people's thinking and opinions matter? If so, consider sharing your work early—even at a lower fidelity than you may be comfortable with.

In the field of user experience (UX), some professionals create very low-fidelity hand-drawn, scissor-cut, taped together paper prototypes of their apps and digital experiences because doing so elicits usability feedback about the "bones" of the experience instead of the superficial characteristics.

In my own career, I had a pivotal moment during my agency years when I relied heavily on designers to make my work more "beautiful," believing that the work would be more persuasive and likely to get "heard" than the translation from brain to slides that I was capable of on my own.

One day, a super high-up global strategy leader I was terrified of called me in on a project with minutes to prepare and no time at all for outside design. I did what I always do: I pulled out a stack of ten sheets of plain paper and a Sharpee marker, and with a few iterations I got my thinking from my head onto the page in rough simple drawings and keywords. Clock ticking, I sat down at my computer and built slides as quickly as I could—but entirely ran out of time. Fully expecting to get fired, I walked back into the leader's office with my stack of physical papers and handed him the pile. He flipped through the pages, asked me a couple of questions, then said to me: "This"—gesturing at the simple drawings on his desk—"is what I want more of from you."

Your smart thinking will sometimes need to be made beautiful for some audiences. But sometimes when you make things too beautiful too early, it alienates collaborators who may feel left out of the co-creation process. It can also tend to elicit critical feedback as if you're presenting a finished product because it looks finished. Starting your socialization of the project with early, rough, low-fidelity prototype can yield better feedback and increased collaborative cooperation and investment.

As you work the exercises in this book, try to practice being intentional in this way. Playing with intentional fidelity might bring with it some illuminating surprises.

Congratulations. If you've completed the suggestions in this chapter, you've got at least a draft of a One-Sheet artifact to inform your effort, including your OKR creation. Great work making good use of that pile of strategic inputs or your own creativity! The most important function of your newly created One-Sheet is clear expectations for yourself, even if you're operating in an organization where expectations are not clearly communicated.

Clear-expectation-challenged organizations

Leaders, baffled when they receive feedback that staff doesn't understand what's expected of them, the organization's strategy, or how their work connects to the strategic priorities, often interpret this as a staff problem—but it's not. It's a signal that the leaders need to look at how clearly communicated those expectations have been.

Leaders often overestimate how clear they are. Even C-Suite and senior executive leaders may be wired for tactics, not strategy. They may lead with a heavy focus on activities, not clear strategic expectations that team members can align to.

In organizations with No-BS OKRs, C-Suite leaders and their seconds are aware that they need to improve expectation clarity.

Leaders

If you receive feedback that reports or colleagues don't understand what's expected of them or the organizational strategy, that is a you problem. It doesn't mean you have to solve it by yourself; it may or may not be one of your strengths to do so. But among your reports, there are inevitably strategically wired people just waiting to jump in. They may be the challenging troublemakers, the ones who always have questions, the ones who are first to point out when there are leaps in logic or exhibit hand-waving behavior about expectations or details. Those troublemakers may turn out to be exactly who you need.

Being strategic is a set of skills that not everyone possesses—sometimes even people who lead may be wired more for tactics than strategies. You need both. The practices you'll learn in this book will make you a better strategic communicator of expectations. The natural-born strategists in your team will benefit from learning the concise, clear, distilled ways to present strategy and strategic alignment clarity that we discuss in this book. The tacticians benefit from these simple practices for elevating your strategic mindset.

Staffers

If you are a staffer in an organization that lacks strategy, the practices in this book enable you to fill those gaps yourself. When expectations are unclear, it may feel impossible to figure out how to succeed. You can create your own One-Sheets and OKRs, then take them to your leadership and ask them to review for alignment.

Don't make them perfect before the review cycle; just get something on the page to give you and your leaders a jumping off point for discussion. In many cases, it may be easier for your leaders to give feedback on your draft than for them to start with a blank sheet of paper. Often, you may set goals for yourself that exceed the goals that your organization has for you.

For example, if you create No-BS OKRs for yourself and your leader says: "What's really most important is that you complete XYZ activity," you can identify those activities as initiatives of importance. You can double check to see is there any success criteria you should aim for. If none are identified, you're free to set your own success criteria that you can then align on. If leadership is not interested in aligning with you about success criteria or outcomes, that's not a you problem.

You can notice the downsides of a leadership lack of engagement on expectations and of leading in ways focused on activity instead of outcomes and take this as a learning for your future leadership career.

TL^DR: STRATEGIST TAKEAWAYS

- Distilling your organization's most important strategic artifacts down to a single page makes it easier for people in your organization to create OKRs in alignment with your strategy.

- Pulling together a Connected Strategic One-Sheet can be done quickly, by anyone, and can provide a significant increase in clarity, focus, and alignment.

- Doing so also derandomizes the key results created by the organization since having examples at the topline of relevant metrics energizes people to think about how their work aligns and what their contributing measures of success might be.

2

WHAT'S POSSIBLE: THE NO-BS HIGH-PERFORMANCE READINESS MODEL

Even early in my work as an OKR consultant, I noticed patterns to the challenges, behaviors, and practices that organizations experienced when trying to shift to more results-focused ways of working, especially with implementing OKRs. Those patterns informed the development of the No-BS High-Performance Readiness Model I now use with clients.

What you see in the figure on the next page is a condensed version I use both to assess the current state of strategic and OKR implementation and to gauge the organization's appetite for progress toward higher performance beliefs and ways of operating.

OKRs are hired to do a job that may require shifting from the left to the right

From	Where would you self-assess your organization?	**To**
We Must Look Good Our performance metrics have to look good, must be within our control, and are spun before presentation.	1 2 3 4 5	We Must Do Better Performance metrics reveal the truth of where we have issues and opportunities so that we can focus on improvement.
Subjectivity Activity and percentage complete goals are common. We're doing all the things, but are not clear on critical outcomes.	1 2 3 4 5	Objectivity We allow empirically measurable progress and success metrics to prioritize activities according to importance of outcomes.
Arbitrary Key Results Everyone has to see themselves in the strategy and OKRs, so non-KRs are included (including run-the-business items).	1 2 3 4 5	Key Results Are Key With rare exceptions, only our most important growth, innovation, and transformation outcomes and measures are key results.
Achievable and Safe We set achievable goals because we lack trust/safety/purpose to stretch ourselves or fear being demotivated by not achieving stretch goals.	1 2 3 4 5	Courageous Experimentation Our strategy and OKRs articulate visionary aspirations for improvement, and we learn by trying (and even failing). Conservative key results are seen as a business risk.
Administrative Strategic planning and OKRs are a "check the box" activity that depends on high coach/admin support.	1 2 3 4 5	Invested And Owned Strategic plans and OKRs are how leaders communicate their vision and expectations. OKRs inform our business decision-making.
Alignment Gap We lack alignment and/or cross-functional cooperation.	1 2 3 4 5	Purpose Alignment We see improvement in "I know how my work matters" scores.

The beliefs and behaviors on the left reflect what I most frequently observe at a new client organization that has tried to implement OKRs but is struggling. The beliefs and behaviors on the right describe a readiness for high performance OKR implementation.

However, not all organizations have the culture or need to land at the far right on every one of those continuums. Since not all organizations share the same aspirations or cultural factors, not all will aspire to the right edge of this readiness model on all factors. Indeed, many organizations find value in occupying the left since even having some direction improves performance compared to having none.

> **Organizations do not jump from the far left to the far right in one step. Each is a building block of progress; making progress on one may advance progress on others.**

The crux of this readiness model is that it can be used to self-assess an organization's current state and then calibrate which of those beliefs and behaviors most need improvement. Then, the organization can intentionally move in the direction they desire in terms of return on investment—in terms of financial investment and labor time—for their strategic planning and OKR implementation. Organizations do not jump from the far left to the far right of this model in one step. Each range is a building block of progress, and making progress on one may begin to advance progress on others.

ASSESS YOUR NO-BS HIGH-PERFORMANCE READINESS

Self-assessment time.

If you have a strategic planning and OKR rhythm presently, complete the below as a self-assessment of your current implementation.

If you're new to strategic planning and OKRs, use it to calibrate your high-performance readiness.

Look again at the previous figure and ask yourself:

- "Of these factors, which ones will make our organization improve its performance the most?"
- "Where does our organization or team [or, where do I] fall on each of these continuums? Does the option on the right sound more like us or the option on the left?"

Mark up a copy of the model reflecting your own implementation's readiness, and then step back and look at the results. Consider:

For each continuum where your organization sits closer to the left:

- Is that working for you? If so, there's no pressing need to change.
- Is that belief or behavior getting in the way of making progress or generating important impacts? Maybe think about moving things to the right.

For each factor where your organization sits somewhere in the middle:

- Will prioritizing change on this factor accelerate progress toward your most important outcomes?
- If your organization would benefit from prioritizing one, two, or three of these factors for improvement, which would they be?

Improvement on each of these factors requires different shifts and changes in different organizations, but there are some patterns to the types of shifts that drive progress.

To develop your own readiness-improvement prescription, look at the example the figure below. This was prepared for an organization that has adopted home-grown OKRs and is running into all the common challenges I often see. They're looking to improve generally, so some factors are more "foundational." They've identified those as P1 priorities for improvement, now. When the organization has some success at those shifts, which may happen quickly once identified, they can move on to the P2 and P3 factors to make further progress.

From	To		By
We Must Look Good	We Must Do Better	p2: Next	Increase number of leading indicators/progress measures in KRs; leaders model "safety to fail"
Subjectivity	Objectivity	p1: Now	No KRs measured subjectively by % complete
Arbitrary Key Results	Key Results Are Key	p1: Now	Reduce OKR volume down to only the most important areas of objective improvement; move RTB and activities to delivery rhythm
Achievable and Safe	Courageous Experimentation	p1: Now	Distinguish between mandatory and stretch measures so people know where they're safe to fail
Administrative	Invested and Owned	p1: Now	Leaders write their own OKRs; coaches and admin support reviews/QAs them
Alignment Gap	Purpose Alignment	p3: Future	Use cross-functional OKRs where necessary in addition to functional OKRs; mature the localization model

When we started, this organization was sitting on the very far left of every continuum on the page, with an appetite to shift right. But culturally they had a very long way to go to achieve a full high-performance implementation. On the far right of the figure, I've included their example prescriptions for each factor. These prescriptions won't work for everyone, but they speak to the biggest repeated issues I see at a broad range of organizations.

It's not wise to focus on all of the continuums at once since trust must be built based on leaders' behavior change and modeling to move right. But some of these factors are critical predecessors. For example, the "P1: Now" items here are all linked; it's not possible for the organization to advance in one without making progress on all of those factors.

I use this same model to enable clients to set goals around which factors are most important to improve. In that case, we add a second set of stars so they can identify where they are and where they hope to be by what date, which, again, clarifies priorities and what beliefs and behaviors must change.

In a high-performance No-BS OKR implementation—designed to achieve transformation, innovation, and change—a few characteristics are common:

- Leaders model the behavior they're asking of the rest of the organization, including all OKR best practices.
- A small number of objectives and key results, at the company level and for any given team or person, indicate that the organization has adequately focused on what's most important to achieve.
- Key results are empirically measurable and give important information about progress and risks that the organization can use to make important business decisions.

* The model makes clear which goals are mandatory; key results are presumptively stretch measures on which they are safe to try (and even fail) in the pursuit of learning and progress.

* Goal owners create their own OKRs; coaches and OKR experts (and administrative support) may provide review and quality assurance oversight, education, and scheduling support, but they do not create OKRs for leaders, teams, or people.

* Key results have a balance of outcome measures (important big goals that may be measured infrequently) and progress measures (that show whether the organization is on or off pace on their outcome measures).

Ultimately, the high-performance organization uses objectives and key results when they're the right tool for the job, and key results are designed to reduce risk and improve performance for projects and initiatives as well as functions and teams. Key results for important cross-functional (a shared responsibility among multiple organizations or teams) outcome and progress measures are also identified, not only functional OKRs within organizational silos.

To have these factors all be true requires a great deal of focus, prioritization, courage, intellectual humility, and a learning culture. This state is not for all leaders or all organizations. But if you're in the business of change, transformation, and innovation,[6] or if your goal is to improve outcomes other than mere revenue, landing on the far

---

[6] No-BS OKRs enable any business to improve overall results, but some industries and organizations may find this approach to have more rigor than their situation requires. Industries that benefit particularly from the No-BS approach are the industries where these approaches specifically developed in my own practice, including healthcare, education, automotive, motorsports, aviation, and adjacent technology organizations. In all of these industries and many others, revenue depends on doing better at the core business—and sometimes human lives depend on that as well.

right of this model builds systemic readiness into your organization and reduces reliance on unicorns and heroism to keep your business on its front foot.[7]

In No-BS OKR high-performance implementations:

- OKRs are experimental.
- Team members are safe to fail.
- OKRs describe shared responsibility.
- Work plans and aligned individual goals describe individual accountabilities.
- Leaders go first.
- Key results in the red elicit comfortable curiosity because that is the learning zone.
- Developing key results in hard-to-quantify territories encourages creativity and collaboration.

[7] Some organizations do manage to stay at the head of their fields or markets without any of these factors being present, often because of an "up market," a charismatic leader, or a talented crew of unicorns or clutch players who keep the business innovating and moving forward. Those factors are subject to change (often rapidly, drastically, and sometimes beyond the control of the organization and its leaders). Adopting OKRs in line with the above characteristics creates systemic, distributed resilience, so that organizations can continue to innovate and transform even in a down market or when key talent moves on (or burns out).

 TL^DR: STRATEGIST TAKEAWAYS

Most organizations have work to do to fully connect their strategy through to implementation. Organizations benefit from:

- Taking stock of their organization's Connected Strategic Stack to understand where OKRs fit into their planning model (and what purpose they're meant to serve).

- Developing a Connected Strategic One-Sheet so that people creating OKRs are working off of the same shared artifact that distills the most important strategic inputs down to one useful document.

- Deciding where on the No-BS High-Performance Readiness continuum to begin (or evolve). Few organizations start at the far right on every measure. But operating guidelines can move organizations toward a more mature, visionary, measurable strategic planning and OKR approach.

THE BIG THINK

The Big Think zooms all the way out and envisions your aspirational world at the end of the current goal cycle. Without a Big Think, you might wind up writing goals for what you already have planned instead of what excites and inspires you.

In my early days as an OKR coach, I used the method I had learned: question participants iteratively about what's most important, why those things matter, and how the participants will quantify progress and impact. But at the end, often teams would step back to look at their final product—and gasp. Someone would realize they'd left out a major objective or key result of critical importance and be gobsmacked that they'd done all this work and forgotten something that important. What was missing from that conventional approach to OKR coaching is the step that takes place before you even begin to think about OKRs. That step is the Big Think.

Once I added the Big Think step, things went a lot smoother. Leaders often tell me that this is the single

> **The Big Think is the single most important step in the process.**

most important step in the process. It gives them a chance to think beyond what's expected or what's urgent and allows space to think about what's important and what might be possible.

THE BIG THINK MINDSET OF NO-BS OKRS

Creating No-BS OKRs for your organization means thinking big about what might be possible. The Big Think lays the groundwork for that vision.

You'll need the courage to craft OKRs to achieve that vision even if doing so is difficult and scary. This requires challenging the status quo and being willing to do things differently—even if you don't yet know how you'll quantify the metrics that matter to you most.

Creating No-BS OKRs means dreaming about the changed future you'd love to see and not letting your inner (or external) critics get in your way. You can create goals for yourself and then learn from trying to achieve them. Whether you "succeed" or "fail," you're gathering important information and learning; no matter what, you can pick yourself up, dust yourself off, and try again in the next cycle.

Here's a special message for leaders:

You now have the opportunity to model vision, courage, accountability, ambition, resilience, trustworthiness, and a host of other beneficial traits and skills to your organization, demonstrated in how you set and lead with OKRs.

You don't have to create your organization's OKRs alone, but you as a leader are responsible for articulating your vision and expectations. OKRs are not anyone else's job; goal setting, clear expectations, and prioritizing are fundamental responsibilities of leadership. It's why you're in the big chair. The buck stops with you on the labor of setting and achieving OKRs, so choose how you collaborate and delegate wisely.

But don't worry! You'll learn practices here to make the OKR elements of your leadership toolkit effective, efficient, engaging, and motivating for yourself and your team.

EXERCISE: TIME TO THINK BIG

In this exercise, you are not yet writing objectives and key results. Instead, you're doing big, aspirational, inspired thinking about what might be possible in your company's next goal cycle. So have at it. Think big and dream a bit about what might be truly awesome or incredible to have come to fruition by the end of this cycle.

Do this exercise quickly, without overthinking. I've observed the magic that comes with the 15–20 minute time limit. It's enough time to activate and warm-up your creative brain; trust that it has been gathering insight for ages and may be very excited for the chance to speak up. Your head will give up what's most important quickly since that often is the first thing that comes to mind. If you ideate for longer, the "shoulds" might start to creep in. Shoulds veer you into business-as-usual territory, which is not where you want to be right now. Resist the shoulds.

Resist the shoulds.

Think big. If you're feeling nervous and excited about the ideas you're coming up with, you're right where you should be.[8]

---

[8] The feeling of experiencing nervousness and excitement at the same time is called "anticipation" in psychological terms. But as a coach who works with clients frequently around mining their peak experiences to yield insight about their strengths and aspirations, I find the word "anticipation" wholly inadequate to describe the power of this sensation. When people experience peak experiences, they often use the words "nervous and excited" or "scared and excited" to describe how they feel. If you're experiencing that powerful sensation while ideating your Big Think, you are in exactly the right place to form OKRs that may lead to your own next peak experiences.

> **Think big. If you're feeling nervous and excited about the ideas you're coming up with, you're right where you should be.**

Step 1: Imagine

Clear your desk, close the door, and set a timer for 15–20 minutes. Imagine yourself 90 days (or a half-year, or a year) in the future and look around.

- What's different?
- What change have you made real?
- What's improved?
- For whom have things improved, and how?
- What are you most proud of?

Write out your answers—don't trust your brain to hold on to them.

Step 2: Assess

After that initial brain dump, take a few minutes to look at what you wrote.

- What are the most important *whats* that emerged?
- If you have more than four or so distinct most important *whats*, can you group them into logical categories or buckets (ideally 3–5 or fewer)?

Step 3: Refine

Now set another 10-minute timer. For each bucket of *whats* ask yourself: "Why does this matter?" If you're not getting beyond "Because we're a business and we have to make money," or "Because I have to," with your *whys*, ask yourself:

- "To whom does it matter the most?"
- "Why or how does it matter to them?"

Step 4: Admire

Now, sit back and admire your work! You likely just ideated around 90% of what may become your OKRs without even breaking a sweat.

CONGRATULATIONS: NOW YOU'RE READY TO CREATE YOUR OKRS

That's it. There is no more pre-work; you've done it all. Well done! At this point:

1. You've learned the most important words and meanings for creating objectives and key results to grow, innovate, and transform.
2. You've ideated your own answers to the most important OKR-forming questions:
   a. What's most important?
   b. Why does that matter (and whose *why* is most important to center, if necessary)?
   c. How do your goals for the upcoming goal term organize into a logical structure and possible themes?
3. And, you've created much of the fodder for your objectives and key results without even thinking about OKRs.

Take a moment to celebrate your progress and get excited about the vision that you have of your potential future.

 TL^DR: STRATEGIST TAKEAWAYS

Use your Big Think to get the most important, most inspired ideas about what might be possible out of your head and onto the page before you start thinking about OKRs. It's hard to draw a map to a future you can't visualize. So take a little time to envision the future you'd like to create so that vision can inform your OKRs.

PART 2

STRATEGIC ALIGNMENT

Imagine being in the bow of a rowboat. You're looking ahead at where you want to go and you're paddling away, but you're not moving very much at all. You paddle stronger and still barely move. Is it the current or a head wind? Is there a paddling technique you haven't yet learned? Are you just fundamentally somehow incompetent at rowing?

You finally turn around and see your rowing partner sitting at the stern of the rowboat, facing behind. They're rowing as hard as they can in the opposite direction. With the best of intentions, perhaps, you've been working against each other the whole time. But since you were both looking where you want to go, not at each other, and not communicating, you were getting nowhere fast.

Sound ridiculous?

This happens every day in the workplace. Well-intentioned, high-achieving people may set their sights in fully opposite directions and not catch the lack of coherence until they've burned valuable time and resources pulling against each other.

Even with a strategy in place to serve as a shared vision, many colleagues engage in a sort of "parallel play"—choosing their toys, then giving themselves a bit of space to focus on their work without the distraction and complication of collaboration.

The pitfalls of an approach like that are self-evident: you waste time, valuable human labor, and resources. You also may experience avoidable frustration with your colleagues, which harms collaboration in the future.

In this part, you're going to learn practices for getting aligned before you kick off your activity so you're more likely to get where you're aiming together.

HOW TO USE THIS PART:

- **Chapter 4: "No-BS OKRs 101"** and **Chapter 5: "OKR Words and Meanings"** provide an introduction into the *whats* and *whys* of No-BS OKRs, with a focus on the often overlooked but critical step of achieving alignment on words and shared meaning.

- **Chapter 6: "Themes"** and **Chapter 7: "No-BS Objectives"** provide an understanding of directional, aspirational, inspired theme-based goals for the small number of big things that merit your deep focus and effort. No-BS objectives cement your direction, so you can maximize your speed in that direction.

- What's most unique and special about OKRs (and hardest for most people to learn) is key results. I've devoted three chapters to key results: to develop your understanding in **Chapter 8: "Deep Dive into No-BS Key Results"**; to learn skills for creating key results in **Chapter 9: "Creating No-BS Key Results"**; and to avoid the common avoidable pitfalls I see in practice in **Chapter 10: "Key Result Mistakes and Pitfalls."**

- **Chapter 11: "OKRs at Scale"** dives into the mechanics of how OKRs move (usually downward) through an organization that's creating them at multiple levels. This chapter is optional—if you're working in an organization that plans to translate OKRs from one level to the next in the organization, this chapter is for you. Otherwise, you can safely skip it.

4

WHAT ARE OKRS?

Ah, the infamous OKRs: Objectives and Key Results. You may have never heard the acronym before this book. If so, you're not alone. While ubiquitous in some corporate environments with global reach and adoption, they're virtually unheard of in others. Or, you may have worked with them already ad nauseum, in management-mandated books, seminars, and workshops; they may have been bandied about for a few cycles without any real traction.

Either way, here you're embarking on something new.

OKRs have been described as "a method for collaborative goal setting and alignment," but this standard definition has its weaknesses, particularly around the use of the concept of goals. Some practitioners argue that thinking about OKRs as goals introduces too much achievement pressure for a practice that depends on continuous learning. When goals are business mandatories for which it's not safe to fail, treating OKRs as goals is problematic.

Others insist that the term "goal" itself is too narrow. Personally, I think of goals as a large universe of all different types of hopes, dreams, and targets—OKRs are a mere subtype. In part, that's based on the dictionary definition of goals (see box). It's also because I have another life in sports in which it's 100% normal to set aspirational goals and work hard toward them (learning in the process) even if you never achieve them. Finally, it's also because my work rests on decades of motivation science research around goal setting.

In practice, well-formed OKRs fill the gap between high-level strategy and tactical implementation so that what your teams do is better aligned with achieving your most important outcomes.

Goal

1. The object or aim of an action.[9]

2. A contributor to high performance by increasing motivation, knowledge and skill development, effort, persistence, and development of knowledge or task strategy.[10]

3. An experiment in how to improve or do better.[11]

So, to share my own definition: OKRs are a goal framework used by organizations to increase **focus, clarity,** and **alignment.**

---

[9]   Locke and Latham, *Goal Setting Theory* (1990), page 4.

[10]   Locke and Latham, *Goal Setting Theory* (1990), page 6.

[11]   This definition is my own, bolstered by a mention in one of my wellbeing coaching texts that defines "goal setting" as "the design of experiments" (Margaret Moore, Erika Jackson, and Bob Tschannen-Moran, *Coaching Psychology Manual*, 2010, 2016, page 162).

- **Focus:** Making deliberate choices about how to deploy limited resources.

- **Clarity:** Being intentional with language choices so that expectations and mutual agreements are clear.

- **Alignment:** Correlating an organization's mission, purpose, and vision with the work its teams do.

Alignment

1. When strategic coordination within an organization ensures collaborators are working effectively toward common goals.

2. When employees' actions and systems are congruent with the organization's strategic progress, demonstrating unity of purpose.

3. When resources and activities are optimized and coordinated, to increase organizational productivity.

4. When the organization works harmoniously, without unnecessary collisions or conflict, as much as possible.

OKRs, initially derived from Peter Drucker's Management by Objectives system, were popularized by John Doerr's 2018 book *Measure What Matters*.[12] That book—widely considered "The

---

[12] *Measure What Matters* was not the first book published about OKRs. Christina Wodke's *Radical Focus: Achieving Your Most Important Goals with Objectives and Key Results* was published in 2016. Wodke's book is written as a parable—walking through a hypothetical OKR adoption in a startup environment. Also published in 2016 was a great technical manual for a foundational approach to OKRs that's still highly regarded among OKR practitioners: *Objectives and Key Results: Driving Focus, Alignment, and Engagement with OKRs*, by Paul R. Niven and Ben Lamorte.

Book" about OKRs based on sales volume—stemmed from Doerr's work with Andy Grove and Google's implementation of OKRs, in addition to other mostly high-tech case studies.

Based on the enthusiasm and buzz that *Measure What Matters* created in the workplace, thousands of organizations worldwide have adopted OKRs, with inconsistent results. In recent years, the over 120 different OKR management software platforms has resulted in additional methodology confusion. Some platforms do a good job of teaching coherent OKR methodology, but some are more focused on selling large software contracts than on the pesky details.

In part, methodology confusion stems from the fact that there is such a range of OKR approaches. Every expert in the field has developed their own definition of what the terms "objective" and "key result" mean.

To be clear: Some organizations can successfully implement the *Measure What Matters* model (or OKRs based on the Google playbook, or any other OKR guide or reference) and have that implementation deliver on the job they hired OKRs to do. But among the change-and-transformation-wired organizations I work with, few were able to achieve an adequate return on time invested based on the *Measure What Matters* or Google playbook models alone.

Doesn't everybody already know what goals are?

It's safe to say that everyone has experience with goals. But every person has a different relationship with goals and goal setting and a different set of beliefs, practices, and heuristics around them. So, two people will rarely speak the same goal language without effort to align.

- Some people approach everything in their life with a vision or goal, then work back from it to inform their choices.

- Some people prefer to make plans and then work forward to achieve what they can.

- Some people have been harmed by the unfair, biased, or incoherent application of goals (especially in the workplace) and may be fearful about goal setting.

- Some free spirits move through the world by winging it, without goals or plans, and manage to thrive.

Even in organizations that have documentation or guidance about their goal model, it's rare for that guidance to coherently connect strategy to implementation in a way that's useful.

So yes, most people know how to write goals, but speaking different goal languages leaves room for expectation/clarity fails, misunderstandings, and misalignments. Even personal or individual goals may involve habits that don't support goal achievement (or joy).

SO WHAT ARE NO-BS OKRS?

Corporate rebels like you and me may not relate to the case studies in books like *Measure What Matters*. A lot of the focus on OKRs has been top down—written to persuade leaders and software buyers of the benefits they'll experience when adopting OKRs—without much attention paid to the potential benefits (or costs) to the people most responsible for whether the company's goals are met: its labor pool. My work with organizations where change is the imperative (not a mere nice-to-have) has yielded a specific flavor of OKRs that features crisp definitions, clear how-tos, and a coherent methodological approach that works whether you're one person or an organization of thousands. I call the result No-BS OKRs.

No-BS OKRs skip the BS that a lot of organizations wade through with do-it-yourself OKRs and jump right to a step-by-step playbook. It emerged from my work mostly with high-change, innovation-oriented, system-transforming organizations where success depends on improving outcomes. The No-BS OKR model is also designed for organizations where improving the bottom line depends on the performance of hard-to-influence outcome measures—like human safety, or health outcomes, or educational outcomes.

Is this system right for you? If you work in an industry where increasing revenue is as straightforward as turning on an advertising budget spigot, the practices in this book may be overkill. If you work in a small/flat organization where it's easier for leaders to maintain alignment with their teams and you don't have big gaps in under-standing between the strategic and implementation layers of your organization, the *Measure What Matters* OKR methodology may work just fine.

> **No-BS OKRs skip the BS and jump right to a step-by-step playbook.**

But when those approaches fail, bring in the practices here. If your current OKR implementation is not working, No-BS OKRs will show you the issues and opportunities for improvement.

Like traditional OKRs, No-BS OKRs are a method for collaborative goal setting and organizational alignment. No-BS OKRs are also a thinking, deciding, and learning practice that achieves greater growth, transformation, and innovation. You'll align on your most important measures of success and progress before you decide on action or activity plans for the goal period.

Most organizations create a durable strategic plan or annual operating plan and then divvy up to decide what to do to support it. In an organization implementing No-BS OKRs, when that strategic or operating plan is created, key stakeholders ask themselves a few additional questions:

- "In our current goal cycle, what might be possible (and incredible) to achieve to advance our strategy?"
- "What would it mean to maximize our success toward our strategy for this goal cycle?"
- "How might we quantify our progress toward that maximum contribution to our strategy? How will we know when we're on or off track?"

Leaders in No-BS OKRs environments ensure that they are aligned on their theory of success and progress before the organization begins implementation, enabling team members to operate based on experimentation, refinement, continuous learning, and improvement. The leaders and do-ers aren't overly attached to pet projects and are aware of the cognitive biases that would keep them pursuing activities that aren't working. No-BS OKR organizations use empirical data to base decisions on; they're unafraid of quantifying goals, success, and progress to improve outcomes, and they're curious and experimental about instrumenting quantitative metrics. Leaders become skilled at recognizing which factual truths must be shared for people in the organization to plan, execute, and monitor the success of their work.

No-BS OKR organizations behave consistently with the deep belief that they're either winning or learning; they know that learning improves the likelihood that they'll

> **No-BS OKR organizations know they're either winning or learning. There must be safety to try and even fail in pursuit of a future win.**

win in the future. To live that ethos, they know there must be safety to try and even fail at their objectives and key results in pursuit of knowledge and experience that will support a future win.

No-BS OKRs are for:

- Thinking deeply about what's most important and what might be possible.
- Identifying which measures of progress and success lead to better decisions in your work and organizations.
- Nurturing curiosity, experimentation, and even "failure" to learn how to improve and grow.

Sound like a lot of work?

Maybe so.

But for some organizations and industries, these are exactly the skills and practices that unlock the transformation necessary for success and impact. For those of us who are wired already for the kinds of practices listed above, finally finding a way to leverage this orientation becomes a sigh of relief in a world of shiny objects and fast tactics.

THE REBELUTIONARY MINDSET

- **Rebelutionary:** A term I coined to describe workplace rebels and revolutionaries who have the audacity to believe that change is possible and that the risks of sticking with the status quo outweigh the risks of experimenting toward progress.

One of the fundamental pillars of creating No-BS OKRs is adopting a Rebelutionary mindset. Specifically, the Rebelutionary mindset values:

- **Vision.** Take the long view on how your business needs to grow, transform, or innovate.
- **Quantifiability.** Measure success through empirical and unbiased data.
- **Doing your best vs. being perfect.** Resist the trap of perfectionism; externalize inspired thinking, prioritize, then get quickly to work.
- **Experimentation.** Don't evaluate only for wins or losses but stay curious and recognize risk-taking and learning.
- **Inspiration.** Remind yourselves of your purpose and tap into your intrinsic motivation with stretch goals and aspirations.
- **Influence, not control.** Encourage naming outcomes you hope to achieve even if they depend on variables beyond your control.
- **Fuel/friction balance.** Know what is motivating you and also assess openly what your frictions or barriers to growth are.
- **Doing better, not looking good.** Focus on achieving improved outcomes and doing quantifiably better, not just making numbers "look good."

Adopting these values will unlock your ability to shift from however you're approaching goals right now to the most fertile mindset for No-BS OKRs.

WHAT ABOUT THINKYDOER TEAMMATES AND CONTRIBUTORS?

- **Thinkydoer:** Another term I coined for people whose work-wiring spans thinking and doing: from insight to idea, through the messy middle, to bring their vision of progress and change to life.

Do you ever find yourself thinking:

- "I wish I understood how to succeed here."
- "What does my supervisor expect of me?"
- "What's wrong with me that the goal posts always seem to be moving?"
- "Does the work I'm doing matter?"

If so, you are not alone. You might be a Thinkydoer.[13]

Thinkydoers are often unconventional leaders, status-quo challengers, and people who find satisfaction in both strategic thinking and pragmatic execution. Deep thinkers and linky-brained people, they are compelled to bring to life the change and improvement they believe is possible in the world.

Disproportionately introverted and neurodivergent (but not exclusively), Thinkydoers are often misunderstood and underserved in dominant business culture. Thinkydoers are status-quo challengers and may feel like square pegs in a round workplace—they may be both brilliant at and struggle or suffer in their careers.

---

[13]   My podcast was originally called "From Think to Do"; I started calling myself and my listeners "Thinkydoers," and it just stuck. I renamed the podcast and haven't looked back.

Some people roll along with working antennae, able to intuit direction from guidance from their leaders—but a lot of us can't do that. If you're one of the many people who struggle to understand expectations in the workplace, No-BS OKRs may clear things up for you tremendously.

While this book is focused on writing organizational OKRs, if you fall into the above category, you also can use many of the same approaches to shape your own goals, both personally and professionally. Once you've identified your own goals, you can proactively share them with your leader for assess alignment and to better understand what's expected of you even if you're the one writing the goals yourself.

TL^DR : STRATEGIST TAKEAWAYS

- OKRs are a goal framework used by organizations to increase focus, clarity, and alignment, filling the gap between high-level strategy and tactical implementation.
  - Focus involves making deliberate choices about how to deploy limited resources.
  - Clarity is about being intentional with language choices so that expectations and mutual agreements are clear.
  - Alignment correlates the organization's mission, purpose, and vision with the work teams do.
- No-BS OKRs skip the confusion and jump right to a step-by-step method, developed working with high-change, innovation-oriented, system-transforming organizations.
- The Rebelutionary mindset is a fundamental pillar of No-BS OKRs, valuing vision, quantifiability, experimentation, and influence over control.

- Everyone benefits from No-BS OKRs, not just leaders. Team members can use No-BS OKRs to create their own clear expectations, even in environments where expectations communicated by colleagues and leaders are not clear.

5

Now that you've wrapped your head around what you're getting into and explored the mindset to approach this work with, let's begin by embracing an essential element of No-BS OKR implementation: agreement on the basic language associated with objectives and key results. A huge accelerator of No-BS OKRs adoption and success is the simple act of aligning on the definitions of these important concept: alignment, outcomes, objectives, and key results.

ALIGNMENT

You can hardly read about OKRs without the word *alignment* coming up in the first paragraph. Alignment is one of the key reasons organizations adopt OKRs, but it's rare for everyone to have the same clear idea of what alignment is.

Let's think about that rowboat again (see the introduction to Part 2). When you and your team are all rowing in the same direction, you're organized, you're headed for the same destination, and you're

Alignment requires clear expectations, shared purpose, a culture of healthy, generative conflict, and pursuit of the same goal.

working together with maximum efficiency. Your activities aren't at odds with each other, and you're reducing wasted effort. In the rowboat situation, if any of the team lacks alignment—if someone rows in the wrong direction and others flail about or don't row at all—you'll have a hard time getting where you want to go.

Alignment requires communication of clear expectations, an understanding of shared purpose, a culture of healthy, generative conflict, and an organization that pursues the same goal.

OUTCOMES

If I could write this book without using the term *outcome* I would. But alas, I fall into the category of OKR experts who depend on this term having meaning. As penance, I'll try to provide a definition to make it less ambiguous and more useful.

The best way to define outcome is to juxtapose it with the more familiar term of activity. Everyone knows what activity is; your activities are the things that you do every day. I get up, I sit down at my laptop, I tell myself today's the day I'm going to finish that to-do list, and then I work until my focus and flow wane. I eat dinner, I get some sleep, and I get up, I sit down at my laptop, and I do the same thing the next day. The balancing of a budget, the building of a product, the service on industrial equipment, the contacting of clients: these labors are work activity.

Are those labors for the sake of mere completion? Sometimes, yes. If a plumber's day involves replacing a broken kitchen faucet, then their labor—their activity—is complete when the kitchen faucet is installed. On to the next activity.

But let's say that plumber made an error when installing the kitchen faucet. Days or weeks later, the homeowner discovers they have a faucet that is askew and leaks. Did the plumber complete their activity? Yes, when they left the homeowner's house the new kitchen faucet had been installed. But what was the homeowner's desired outcome? To have a new faucet installed or to have one that worked?

This is the distinction between activities and outcomes. Installing the faucet was the plumber's activity. The desired outcome of the installation was a working faucet. The activity can be complete without the outcome having been achieved.

Most people are wired for creating goals around their activity. People feel a sense of control over activity that they don't have when it comes to outcomes. The outcomes of activity are affected by numerous variables, some that may be in your scope of influence and some that may be wholly beyond your control. Perhaps the plumber made a mistake with the kitchen faucet installation. Perhaps the seals the plumber pulled out of the kit had been packed incorrectly at the faucet factory, leaving the plumber with fittings that didn't fit that particular faucet but no way to know that was the case.

> **The distinction between activities and outcomes is that the activity can be complete without the outcome having been achieved.**

Is the plumber excused from responsibility for the leaking sink, just because they didn't control all of the variables of the installation? Usually not. In a customer-service-oriented culture, activity and labor often has some kind of success criteria that dictates the standards by which successful completion can be measured. In the OKR scenario, those success criteria give an idea of how you would empirically evaluate completion in the form of outcomes.

You'll read over and over in most leading OKR sources that objectives and key results should describe outcomes, not activity. Sadly, those same sources often go on to show example key results that quantify activity rather than empirically measurable outcomes. This is confusing. But here in No-BS OKR land, OKRs are designed to describe outcomes, not activities.

Part of the challenge here is that the word *outcome* itself is ambiguous. The argumentative can fairly assert that completing an activity a certain number of times has an outcome: that activity is now complete, and that completion is the outcome. So here, let's turn to the trusty dictionary for a fact-check.

One definition in Merriam Webster for outcome is: "something that follows as a result or consequence." Rather than considering completion of activity an outcome, the dictionary encourages you to consider the result or consequence of that activity.

Thinking in terms of outcomes can be quite difficult, especially for people who have been harmed by environments with unclear expectations or moving goal posts. The shift requires you to imagine a future that doesn't exist yet, where you do not control all of the variables that may affect outcome achievement. That in itself is a mindset that must be cultivated.

Practice this thinking on your own, routinely. When you stand at the sink washing dishes, what's most important? Completing the washing of the dishes (activity) or the sparkling clean kitchen ready for you to make your next meal in (outcome)? You can notice which thought inspires you more to work toward task completion or goal pursuit. Some people are more naturally wired for the tactical and will be more motivated by the thought of completing the task. Some are naturally wired for vision, where washing the dishes may be wholly uninspiring but the vision of the gourmet meal you can make thanks your sparkling clean kitchen may be the inspiration behind being willing to do the task. Neither is better than the other; both the activity and the desired outcome are important. Whichever way you lean, you can practice developing your toolkit for your non-default mode.

Reading a book? Activity. Becoming competent at the new skill the book teaches? Outcome.

Clearing your overgrown yard of blackberry bramble? Activity. Hosting backyard barbecues with your closest family and friends thanks to your presentable backyard? Outcome.

Launching the latest version of your new product? Activity. Achieving a five-star rating from early adopters in the first two weeks after launch? Outcome.

Answering a customer support inquiry? Activity. Resolving the customer support inquiry so they recommend you to their friends? Outcome.

This is the mental skill that you'll cultivate through the course of this book. You are probably already skilled at identifying and planning activities; your organization may even have project managers and project management software that operationalizes that step. It's the next step of asking yourself, "What is the result or consequence we hope our activity achieves?" That's your outcome, and that's what you'll build the muscle to identify through the exercises in this book.

OBJECTIVES AND KEY RESULTS, DEFINED

Something interesting from my teaching OKR coaching is how often students tell me that it's valuable (and unique) that I teach objectives and key results as two separate things. Apparently, OKRs are sometimes thought of and treated as a monolith: OKRs—all one word—as a single concept. But OKRs are two separate terms, with their own special meanings.

Often when OKR implementations aren't working, it's because these words have been allowed to mush together. Team members spend cognitive bandwidth trying to understand or debate the methodology when they can and should be focused on goal setting, achievement, and learning.

I've also seen organizations devote endless cycles of discussion to what certain words mean: Is an objective a goal? Is a goal an objective? What's the difference between a goal and an objective? In my experience, such philosophical discussions were often (perhaps subconsciously) a delay tactic due to anxiety about goal setting, not actual attempts to learn and understand the methodology.

So let's get this straightened out. Here's a straightforward definition of OKRs themselves:

- **OKRs:** Transformation and alignment methodology that relies on two major parts: objectives and key results. OKRs represent your company's current theory about the outcomes and progress you are aiming for, to further your strategy. Fully mature OKRs serve as a measurement model to empirically evaluate your progress and success and learn from your setbacks.

Later, objectives and key results will get deep-dive treatment when it's time to talk about creating each, but for now, let's cover some quick definitions so you can begin to think about objectives and key results as separate tools to leverage for different purposes.

WHAT ARE OBJECTIVES?

- **Objective:** An ambitious statement of shared purpose, providing direction and focus for your efforts during the current goal cycle. Objectives are often like "mini vision statements"; each one is a pillar of support for your strategy. Objectives may be created for themes or initiatives.

Objectives are directional (usually not measurable) purpose statements, describing what you're pursuing as an organization and why it matters (and sometimes, to whom it matters most).

A few example objectives:

> Earn back our market-leading customer trust to provide a firm foundation for growth.

> Become the go-to resource to alleviate Chief of Staff overwhelm.

> High-satisfaction talent creates inspired products that leads to a brighter future.

Objectives serve as a container for key results so you can focus on a few essential directions. I recommend that a working group or an organization have no more than two to five objectives at a time.[14] Personally, I aim for up to four in any single set of OKRs; up to four fit nicely on one sheet of paper so you can always keep them in view and therefore top of mind.

---

[14] A recent interview with Ben Lamorte recommended two minimum: one internal, one external, which is sound advice.

Traditional OKRs	Most sources coach that groups should create 3–5 objectives.
No-BS OKRs	Create only the objectives that are essential: may be as few as one for some teams; but at the organizational level 2–5 ensure that you have objectives about both your internal and external goals. Organizationally, there is often a sweet spot with four objectives, since that enables one objective each about the following important themes: · Growth/financial health · Operational improvement · Customer and product · Talent and culture

There are many different structures for objectives, but the formula I advocate starting with is a *what/why* objective. They're quicker to write than other forms; they're clear on their face without needing a lot of additional explanation or context; and they provide an answer to the two most important objective-forming questions:

- What's most important to achieve?
- Why does that matter?

The building blocks of a *what/why* objective are:

[What's most important to achieve] + [why it matters]

A couple of example objectives might be:

Create an inspired, empowered work culture so
our people can wow every customer interaction.

Release Product XYZ to maximize buzz and
positive reputational impact.

Objectives: summed up

Objectives are like mini vision statements. They describe the small number of important directions you're looking to improve and typically answer the question of what's most important and why that matters.

WHAT ARE KEY RESULTS?

- **Key result:** An aspirational, empirically measurable target that clarifies the most important measures of progress and success towards achieving an objective. Ideally key results are a blend of: quantifiable outcomes that may be a lagging or binary metric, and progress metrics (leading indicators) so you can assess your progress and risks as you work.

Key results are your most important empirically quantified (measurable) aspirational targets that define the progress and success you're aiming to achieve. A few examples:

Increase employee retention by 30 points (from
60% to 90%).

Improve our product development process efficiency
index score by 20% (from 80% to 96%).

Increase the rate at which we hear positive spontaneous statements about "ease" in customer feedback by 10x (from 3x weekly to 30x weekly).

What's universally stated by OKR experts is that key results should describe your most important outcomes and not your activities. Unfortunately, many of these selfsame experts will then show examples of key results that are nothing but activities. If you start by including activities (including milestones[15]) in your key results, it's really hard to know when and where to stop. This lack of discipline can lead to having way too many OKRs.

When I begin working with a new team, often the vast majority of what they're calling key results are either quantified activity (do a thing X times) or milestones (launch a thing by X date). That's my cue to work with them to narrow the criteria for activity to be considered a key result and to keep their key results as empirically measurable as possible.

Traditional OKRs	No-BS OKRs
· Key results may be milestones or measurable goals that you can look at and without any arguments ask and answer: "Did I do that or did I not do it?"[16]	· Key results are empirically measurable and describe progress (leading indicators) or outcomes (lagging results).

---

[15] Milestones are a type of mandatory commitment where X must happen by Y date.

[16] Andy Grove, quoted by John Doerr in *Measure What Matters*, page 23.

Traditional OKRs (cont'd)	No-BS OKRs (cont'd)
· Most modern mainstream sources agree that key results should describe outcomes, not outputs or activities, but then many approaches permit key results that quantify activity (e.g., "Do [activity] [X] times," which describes an output, not an outcome). · Most sources coach 4–6 key results per objective.	· If there isn't a number in it, it's not a key result, *unless* it's a baseline activity (the outcome of which is a baseline number, not the activity itself). · Milestones are not key results, since milestones are typically mandatory goals; key results are by definition stretch. · With No-BS OKRs, use the smallest number of key results possible to reflect the most important progress and success measures. For any given working unit (organization, team, project), the total number of key results should be manageable and memorable. Often this means 2–5 key results per objective.

Key results are specific quantifiable goals with targets that you're prioritizing for focused achievement. You can think of each key result as a theory or experiment in how you might do better.

In the No-BS OKR model:

- You will work to create a safe environment to craft aspirational and inspired key results around goals that you influence but don't control since that is how to achieve more than incremental change to the status quo.

- You and your colleagues will work together to more creatively and empirically measure or quantify your progress and impact by envisioning the outcome your effort may achieve and what signal lets you know you're on or off track.

- Meaningful key results often require instrumenting new metrics or creatively using signal data (like observation, or listening) outside of traditional business analytics platforms. You won't start with "What can we measure?"—those are most likely KPIs. You will start with "What's most important to achieve? How will we know empirically that we're making progress?" even if you can't yet measure your progress today.

New practitioners of OKRs tend to go straight to the metrics they have available already—whatever instrumented metrics are available in their business tools today—rather than thinking about what's important to quantify in terms of progress or success. This leads to confusion between KPIs and key results when the two are distinct. KPIs are the maintenance measures that you keep an eye on to ensure your business is healthy; key results are your stretch goals that set a target for what it might mean to succeed wildly.

After KPIs, people tend to go straight to the activities or milestones they have planned. I ask a few questions to move their thinking beyond activity and into outcomes:

- When you do [activity] [X] times, how will you know you are successful?
- When you launch [activity] by [X] date, what would it mean to succeed wildly?
- While you're doing [activity] [X] times, what will indicate that you're on the right track?
- While you're working to launch [activity] by [X] date, how will you empirically know you're making progress?

The answers to those questions may yield ideas for key results that give better direction about how to work during the goal term and what success might mean than just describing planned activities.

Traditional Key Results		
Repackage the entire 8086 family of products (Marketing).[17]	Sample the arithmetic coprocessor no later than June 15 (Engineering).[18]	Source one product marketing manager (meet with five candidates this quarter).[19]
Why It's Not a No-BS OKR		
The verb (repackage) is not an empirically quantifiable target.	The date indicates this is a milestone. Milestones are mandatory goals not aspirational/stretch.	Including two numbers makes it unclear which is more important to consider with this KR. It's also quantifying activity, not outcomes.
No-BS OKR Key Results		
The repackaging of the 8086 family of products decreases customer decision time to purchase by 30 days (from 60 days to 30 days).	Sampling the arithmetic coprocessor decreases errors in Product X compilation by 30% (from 9/day to 3/day).	New hire product marketing manager achieves a score of 9/10 on first 30-day new hire evaluation.
Why It's a No-BS OKR		
What's important is the outcome (decreasing customer decision time), not the activity (the repackaging).	What's important is the desired outcome (decreasing errors in compilation), not the completion of the task without success criteria identified.	A single metric makes this measurable and focuses on the ideal outcome (a great new hire), not mere completion of the activity of recruiting and hiring.

[17]   *Measure What Matters*, page 42, Intel Key Result from Q2 1980.

[18]   *Measure What Matters*, page 42, Intel Key Result from Q2 1980.

[19]   *Measure What Matters*, page 66, example old Twitter Key Result.

When you land on a key result candidate, you do a last check:

1. Is this one of the most important progress measures for this goal term? Or,
2. Is this a justification for a planned activity or goal for a specific project or team?

The former is an organizational key result. The latter may be a key result for a project or initiative but does not belong in your organizational key results. These quality-check gates are how you keep organizational key results prioritized and focused on the smallest number of most important performance indicators that you require objective data to understand.

In No-BS OKRs, I encourage writing key results as outcome-based goals and leading indicators to give you data about whether you're on or off track as you pursue outcomes. Recognize that you don't necessarily control the outcome of every key result—your key results are going to take you into new and uncertain territory. But your naturally terrible estimating powers as a human being are at even more of a disadvantage if you have too many unknowns to forecast with any certainty. While you may hope to influence the outcome of your key results, they're measures of progress and success important enough for you to aim for even if you don't know you can achieve them. They are stretch measures of the progress you aspire to. If you achieve them, you celebrate; if you don't, you take stock and run a new key result experiment in the next goal cycle.

Key results are important to aim for even if you don't know you can achieve them.

The basic "textbook" formula I coach for key results is:

[Increase/decrease/improve] [a metric] by [X%] from [Y] to [Z]

This formula works because:

1. The initial verbs are directional; they indicate a number is going to move.
2. What they're looking to change is not an action but a metric, measure, or observable behavior.
3. The measure of success is actual numbers that change from a start value to a finish value.

Voila! You cannot complete this formula without putting a number in your key result.

In my experience, this formula solidly ensures that you're writing an empirically measurable key result instead of quantifying an activity or a milestone.

Here are two examples of key results written in that textbook form:

- "Increase CSAT by 50% (from 6 to 9)."
- "Increase the frequency with which we hear spontaneous feedback from our customers about how delightful their experience with one of our associates was by 3x (from twice a week to six times per week)."

Q: Does the key result ever include the why?

A: While *why* plays a very important role in objectives (inspiring people by linking what's most important to shared purpose), it is not included in the key result formula. It's hard enough to get people to focus on writing measurable key results when that's all you include in them. There's no reason that you can't include a *why*. But I tend to not include it because it isn't strictly required for a key result to be empirically measurable.

Q: Does the key result ever include the how?

A: It can feel natural to include what you plan to do even when you're writing a quantifiable-outcome-focused key result. An example might be: "Implement virtual reality to increase our efficiency on customer support satisfaction by X% (from A to B)."

If it's important is that you use VR to achieve the result, you can include it. However, when you clutter the key result with extra detail, it focuses on the purpose of the activity—its *why*, which doesn't need to be there—and you may forget to put in the important detail of quantified impact.

Summary

This is not to say you'll never include a *how* or a *why* in a key result. There are times when you want to communicate these to implementers. But as a rule, if you focus on the metric, measure, or behavior that you want to change, predetermining the *how* and distracting with the *why* can hamstring or confuse implementers.

Key results: summed up

Key results are your experiments in quantifying the improvement you seek. They make clear what quantifiable improvements are your most important measures of progress and success.

THE NO-BS OKRS LOOP

What I'll be sharing in the following chapters is a simple and replicable method that evolved from my years both as an OKR coach and someone who creates OKRs for my own businesses, work, and life. It's also informed by trying a few methods that did not work.

In time, you'll also figure out what works best for you. Even within this step-by-step, you'll see there are many options. Leaders of large, highly matrixed enterprises may wind up with objectives and key results similar to solopreneurs, but they may have very different strategic inputs and accountabilities. So, this exploration will have some elements of choosing your own adventure. Enjoy!

Steps for high quality, useful NO-BS OKRs:

Step 1: Review your strategic artifacts and develop your Connected Strategic One-Sheet, collecting any potential measures you notice in your parking lot.[20]

Step 2: Think before you write; complete a Big Think.

Step 3: Create your objectives.

Step 4: Create your key results.

Step 5: Then optionally, identify initiatives that align to your OKRs and create initiative key results for the most important ones if needed.

Step 6: Use all this as an artifact for informing the process again in your next cycle.

---

[20] This first step may also include completing a retrospective (I call them Learning Reviews). If in your case it's important that you not only understand your strategic inputs but also assess recent performance for learning that may affect your OKRs, you can insert a Learning Review in between Steps 1 and 2 here. Learn more about Learning Reviews in Chapter 15: "Implementing OKRs" and you can find my Learning Review worksheet in the No-BS OKRs Workbook.

From there, OKRs can be 1) reviewed for quality and alignment, 2) communicated, and 3) localized into the organization for teams and initiatives.

Each of these steps will have its own chapter, but here is some context about the first two that may save you some confusion and frustration (and possibly allow you a few shortcuts).

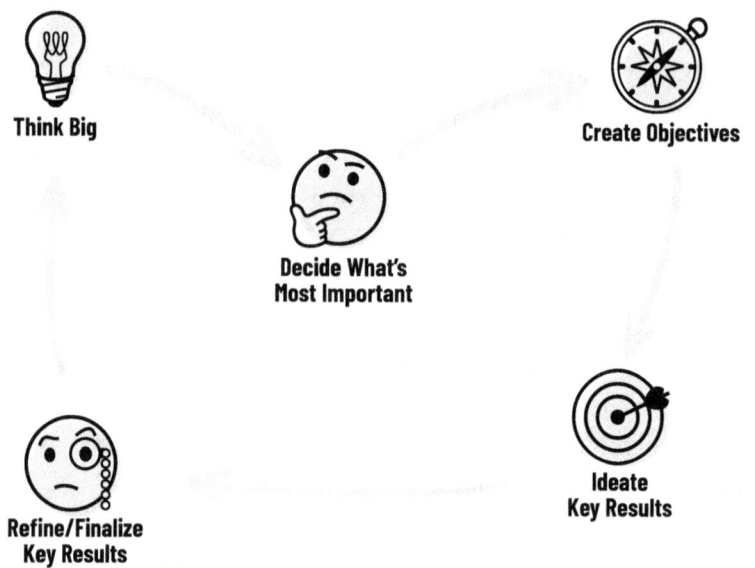

Think Big

Decide What's Most Important

Create Objectives

Ideate Key Results

Refine/Finalize Key Results

THAT'S AN INFINITE LOOP. WHERE DO I START?

Typically, the first step in creating OKRs from scratch is to either: triage strategic artifacts and create your One-Sheet as in Chapter 1: "Making Strategy Usable and Useful"; or begin with your Big Think.

Reviewing your strategic artifacts is important if you are responsible for delivering on an upline strategy for upline or outside stakeholders. If you are responsible to an entity like a board of directors;

if you report to a boss or senior executive; or if you are responsible to a market to whom forecasts or promises have been made, reviewing strategic artifacts is essential. This step is also important if there is an upline strategy that your work should support (whether or not it's in the form of upline objectives and key results) or an annual operating plan or other document that spells out expectations.

If you are a solopreneur or an individual sitting down to create OKRs for yourself and there is not a larger strategy or upline or outside stakeholders, you may have skipped that step, and can move on to Chapter 3: "The Big Think" to begin your Big Think. But make that decision carefully: you might find great value from creating a quick One-Sheet to provide some strategic direction to your Big Think.

TL^DR: STRATEGIST TAKEAWAYS

- Alignment is crucial for OKR success, requiring clear communication, shared purpose, and a culture of healthy conflict to ensure everyone is working towards the same goal.

- Outcomes are the results or consequences of activities. They are influenced by many variables, and represent what you aim to achieve.

- Objectives are aspirational statements that provide direction and focus, often serving as mini vision statements for themes or initiatives.

- Key results are empirically measurable stretch goals that measure progress and success towards achieving objectives.

- OKRs are a methodology for transformation and alignment, representing the company's theory about the outcomes and progress aimed for to make the largest possible contribution to the larger strategy for the current goal term.

- A textbook key result is typically written in alignment with the following formula:
  - [Increase/decrease/improve] [metric/measure/observable behavior] by [change percentage or points] from [start value] to [finish value].
- To make creating and achieving OKRs as efficient as possible, follow the cycle of No-BS OKR creation shown in the illustration in **Chapter 15: "Implementing OKRs."**

6

THEMES

Most objectives can be categorized by a short keyword theme—think financial health, innovation, or operating efficiency—that communicates unmistakably the business focus an objective aligns to. Identifying important themes before creating objectives brings focus to ideation, especially in organizations that will be localizing OKRs down into the organization.

As mentioned before, when I bring up objective themes in coaching, once I explain what they are, how we use them, and the purpose they serve, someone will speak up and say: "So, they're like the 'buckets' that our OKRs arrange into?" Yes! That's *exactly* what they are.

There is no right time to decide on themes; theme identification may take place at many stages of OKR creation (or not at all). If you are creating a single OKR for an initiative or yourself, you may skip the objective theme section and move on to Chapter 7: "No-BS Objectives." However, if you're creating a set of OKRs that has multiple objectives, it's good to process this building-block up front.

> **Themes communicate what's most important and distinctive about that objective compared to the others in a multiple-objective set of OKRs.**

Themes communicate what's most important and distinctive about that objective compared to the others in a multiple-objective set of OKRs. They preserve internal alignment in organizations that carry OKRs down multiple layers since the different objectives that teams may devise still should align to the same theme.

Some people find that establishing a range of themes avoids the later problem of over-indexing on one part of the business (usually growth and revenue) while neglecting important contributors (like customer experience, employee satisfaction and culture, and operational excellence).

Some typical themes are:

- Growth/financial health
- Customer experience
- Product development
- Innovation
- Operational improvement
- Employee experience (or people and culture)

Select which ones your organization needs to improve on or identify your own that best align to your business. Then you can go on to ideate an objective for each theme.

Example Company OKRs

Objective Themes

01: Influence

Become a trusted source of behavioral insight and practical/applied resources among people working with or considering OKRs.

KEY RESULTS

1. Increase word of mouth measured by 10x social media unprompted mentions of brand terms (from 0/month to 10/month)
2. Increase strongly positive feedback responses by 14% (from 46% to 60%)
3. Increase brand content post amplification by 10x (from 1/month to 10/month)

Objectives

02: Good Growth & Financial Health

Shift from services to a blend of products and services to increase the number of people we can help.

KEY RESULTS

1. Increase inbound lead contacts for non-course products and services by 10x (from 1/mo to 10/mo)
2. Increase % of revenue from services vs products by 22% (from 3% to 25%)
3. Automate early inquiry sales nurture to reduce loss rate after custom proposal from 3 to 1 per year

Avoid ideating myopically about the themes, though. Always lead with the essential question:

"What's most important to achieve, and why does it matter?"

If themes don't apply to a part of the organization that is more an initiative or executional level, there may not be the authority to create transformation around themes like those listed above. It's always worth asking the question:

"Do I have room for improvement on any of those
themes, and is making that improvement within
my influence?"

If so, try creating one objective for the theme that's most impactful
or important for you to improve on. Then your other OKRs can be
treated as initiatives, which we'll look at in more detail in **Chapter 12:
"Identifying Initiatives."**

"Do I need to worry about objective themes?"

Organizing by theme:

- **Focuses your objectives.** Even a *what/why* objective benefits
  from having a one or two word theme as a summary of its
  territory for improvement.
- **Brings you into alignment.** When you have clarity about the
  themes you're working to improve, teams can create their
  own objectives in alignment with the upstream themes (for
  when the upstream objectives aren't as relevant to that
  team but the themes may be).
- **Organizes your key results.** Occasionally you'll have an important key result that doesn't align to the specific language
  in your objective but that's still of critical importance. If
  your objective has an identified theme, then the key result
  can be aligned to that theme (even if not perfectly to the
  objective language itself).
- **Gives clarity.** If your objective can't be aligned to a one- or
  two-word theme, it may be too general or broad to be
  meaningful. You may discover this when you begin writing
  key results and have a hard time figuring out which objective they align to.

When I create my own organization's objectives, sometimes I start with themes, sometimes I don't. Sometimes I start with an all-up exploration of what's most important for us to achieve. I don't think one way is better than the other. If this tool works for you, use it.

At the company level (e.g., the top level OKRs for an organization), themes clarify and organize objectives.

On a team level, thinking about the typical themes listed above may inspire thinking about parts of the work that need improvement but that may not be top of mind. If you're working at a team level and you don't feel the team has any influence over those themes, double-check yourself. Could this team's work improve the product experience? Improve the customer experience? Yield increased operational efficiency? If so, try creating an OKR for that theme.

If you're creating goals for a purely executional part of the organization, you may find it challenging to create objectives aligned to themes at all. In that case, skip the themes, identify important initiatives, and create OKRs aligned to those initiatives.

TL^DR: STRATEGIST TAKEAWAYS

- Themes enable objective focus, clarity, and OKR alignment.
- At the company level, common themes include growth/financial health, customer experience, product development, innovation, operational improvement, employee experience (or people and culture).
- Teams may have their own discipline-specific themes in addition to the above.

- Identifying themes prior to ideating *what/why* objectives encourages systematically thinking through the various parts of your business.
- If you're creating goals by theme, make sure you do a big picture, holistic check-in on what's most important and why it matters to avoid missing any big, important *whats* and *whys*.

7

NO-BS OBJECTIVES

Congrats! You've completed your Big Think and optionally considered your themes. It turns out that if you asked yourself the *what* and *why* questions, you may already have ideated a good bit of the language you'll need to create your objectives.

WHAT MAKES OBJECTIVES SUCCESSFUL?

Successful objectives are clear, memorable, and useful. They typically can be recited in one breath when spoken out loud. Too many clauses, too many commas, and you may have objective "word salad"—the opposite of clear, memorable, and useful.

It's important that objectives are carefully chosen. I coach the theme identification work before crafting objectives to zero in on important territories before drafting objectives themselves. Most organizations can only afford to make progress in a certain number of directions at a time, so the number of objectives should be limited to three or four, or one objective for a major initiative/theme.

Objectives typically have a time horizon of more than one quarter, although this may vary, especially with initiative OKRs.[21] Objectives may span one or more years, quarters, or sprints, and occasionally are written to persist until achieved. That lets you elevate your thinking above the tactical so that you are describing the direction of travel that's most important (not just urgent) with an aspirational lens.

No-BS objectives are directional and, counterintuitively, not measurable.[22] Measurable goals are better framed as key results. If you place a key result in the objective slot, not only are you flying in the face of the words and their meanings but also often that so-called objective will yield key results of its own that are tasks, not outcomes.

> **No-BS objectives communicate what is important and why it matters.**

No-BS objectives serve as visionary pillars that hold up the organization's larger strategy. Added together, they describe what's most important to achieving your larger strategy.

No-BS objectives communicate what is important and why it matters. The most compelling objectives describe their *why* in human terms.

Lastly, No-BS objectives are written to be useful. They're short enough to be memorable. When you run into a conflict or difficult decision, you can look at your objectives to break deadlock or

---

[21] See Chapter 12.

[22] There are exceptions: Every once in a while, a lofty aspirational measurable or quantifiable objective is merited. There's a famous example of an objective at Google around YouTube minutes viewed that was a lofty aspirational long-term goal where it did make sense to have supporting key results aligning to that goal in order to help the organization achieve it.

determine how to move forward. The word choice in your objectives is important (although avoid wordsmithing too much; see below) since individual words create opportunities for cross-functional alignment or metrics. In other words, the words in your objective might give you ideas about your most important success measures.

There are a few simple examples of objectives:

> NewProduct 2.0 launches with a customer experience so delightful our users can't wait to tell their friends.

> Restore an internal culture of excellence: high integrity, no shortcuts, only the truth.

> Keep the team healthy and operating at top performance by improving nutrition and sleep habits.

Each is clear about what's important and why it matters; each is complete enough to be meaningful but short enough it can be read out loud in a single breath. Each includes enough information to know what's important, but not so much that the objective is trying to be everything to everyone.

EXERCISE: CREATING OBJECTIVES STEP BY STEP

If you're creating OKRs for an organization or team, you may need to create more than one objective—usually one for each bucket you identified in your themes and Big Think work. As mentioned earlier, I recommend aiming for four or fewer. This indicates a healthy level of focus and prioritization, and four or fewer fit nicely on a single page so it's easy to keep them top of mind.

Creating a single objective for each initiative—important collaborative workload[23]—can increase shared understanding significantly. Your *what* is the initiative, and the *why* yields increased clarity and alignment for everyone who works on it.

Even if you're only creating OKRs for yourself, as an individual, I'd coach you to keep the number of objectives small and focused. No matter how ambitious you are when you're goal setting, if each objective is setting a direction, you can only head in so many directions at once.

Step 1: Gather input

Set a timer for 20–30 minutes, and look at your One-Sheet and Big Think for any potential inspiration for possible outcomes.

- What are the logical conclusions those artifacts suggest?
- Have any *what/why* pairs risen to the top level as "umbrella" statements of your intent and aspiration?
- Can you identify a draft *what/why* statement for each of your most important themes?

Again, the two questions I typically ask to develop objectives are:

- What is most important to achieve?
- Why does that matter?

---

[23]   More on identifying initiatives and creating initiative OKRs is in Chapter 12: "Identifying Initiatives."

You have a head start on these questions already from your Big Think. Notice any Big Think language that might inform your objectives?

- Look for language that sits at the level of a mini vision statement that describes what's important for you to achieve.
- Look for language in your *why* statements that might be important for communicating your shared purpose.

Sometimes, the building blocks for objectives are right in that first batch of externalized thinking. If not, mine it for what you can, then re-ask yourself the questions above about each of your objective themes. Collect your thoughts about what's important and why it matters, and look for language in your ideation that is especially clear or meaningful.

Step 2: Narrow the choices

Narrow your goal themes or initiatives down to three or four max at the organizational level or one or more initiatives if you're a project manager or work deep in implementation.[24] By the end of this exercise, aim to have one to four draft objectives that will sit as your "top level" objectives.

---

[24] That said, I would argue that almost any working group and person can align to important themes around financials and growth, operational excellence, customer, product, innovation, or people and culture, so it never hurts to try.

Step 3: Refine with what/why

Use this framework to create your actual objective phraseology.

[What's most important to achieve] + [why it matters]

Asking those questions yields objectives like:

Laser focus on experience to win vocal brand love

Increase efficiency so we can maximize instead of making painful cuts

Increase cross-functional alignment so we can move at the speed our customers expect of us

The *what/why* objective answers the two most important questions collaborators have: what direction they're responsible for heading in together, and what's important about how they work based on the *why*.

WORD TO THE WISE: AVOID WORDSMITHING

Overworking or wordsmithing your objectives burns time and at best yields an objective that's only incrementally better than your rough draft. At worst, it yields an objective that's been massaged into nonsense.

My early OKR coach training taught me to spend about half of the time creating objectives and about half of the time creating key results. Since then, I've found that when objective writing was treated as a collaborative project, teams never had enough time to discuss their way to an final version—and they were very uncomfortable moving on to key results.

I also saw many collaborative drafting sessions yield cute, catchy, tagline-style objectives that served as memorable rallying cries:

Profit sustains us; it doesn't define us

Big-up our growth potential

Customer experience perfection

Teams are often coached to develop rallying cries or taglines because they're catchy, concise, and memorable. They're easy to throw out in conversation during a conflict or crisis. However, when catchy objectives are shared with an extended team in a big executive announcement, colleagues often respond with puzzled looks and ask: "But—what does that mean? What's important? And why does it matter?"[25]

Noticing that pattern, I changed my approach. To get to a draft objective quickly with enough alignment that you can move into key result setting, use the steps above to quickly draft a candidate objective. You can always come back to it and work on a catchy tagline after the fact, if you like. But keep your *what/why* handy, since it explains the tagline to your colleagues and stakeholders.

---

[25] This isn't to say we *never* use tagline-style objectives. My motorcycle racing team had an objective one year of "We make every grid." It was one of our most frequently recited reminders throughout the season when we had difficult decisions to make and was a highly effective tie-breaker when faced with some of our most challenging decisions. We would never compromise rider safety. But we definitely did make the grid in many situations where it was expensive or risky (from a business standpoint) to do so, thanks to that objective.

MINIMUM VIABLE PRODUCT RUBRIC

Another tactic for writing objectives is the minimum viable product (MVP) objective. I became acquainted with the term "MVP" in software development and creative agencies, where an MVP is the simplest possible version of a product or deliverable that can be released to the market to test product/market fit or to gather learnings from users without the overhead and investment of building a finished product. The purpose of an MVP is to develop just enough to test product/market fit and to be usable enough that users can test and provide feedback for future development.

Create an MVP objective that clearly answers the two questions above and then get to work. You'll improve your objectives by seeing what you learn working with them than by trying to perfect them through wordsmithing.

Data is neutral information, not to be afraid of

One of the biggest mindset shifts this work has surprised me with (which I still struggle to remember) is that data is helpful, neutral information, not something to fear. If you're wired for perfectionism, you might tend to overthink, well, everything. This can lead to long cycles of thinking and planning while you try to create a plan that you're confident enough about to put into action.

Yes, some things merit long cycles. But your "long thinking and planning" muscles might just have become overdeveloped through overuse and become your hammer in the old "if you have a hammer, everything looks like a nail." You may have developed a habit of overthinking and overplanning. There is another tool for the job: your "move fast and learn things" muscles.

For many things in life and work, long thinking and planning cycles increase instead of decrease anxiety. They can take you out of the present moment and into an unknown and unknowable future, which further increases anxiety. The more you think and plan, the more scenarios fractal outward in your brain, leading to an exponential number of scenarios that then haunt you until they're resolved—but they just keep multiplying. It becomes hard to know when to stop.

During my early strategy career, I serendipitously learned to stop when I noticed the pattern emerging,[26] but patterns emerge when you have data, not imagined scenarios.

The earlier in your process you can begin to gather data—neutral information that can inform learning, experimentation, and decision-making—the better.

Instead of long cycles of thinking and planning followed by an anxious implementation that may not live up to the expectations your lengthy and comprehensive deliberation has set for yourself, is there a test or experiment you can run now to gather data to inform your way forward?

This process of developing a theory quickly, testing it, gathering data, learning and improving—*that* is No-BS OKRs.

You may have heard the phrase "building in public," which means showing your work—even the messy parts and the failures—while you're creating it. It feels scary, especially if you struggle with perfectionism or anxiety. But curiosity is an antidote to anxiety. By building in public or launching an MVP before you feel ready, you gather data—neutral information—to be curious about. Some of it may be helpful and make you feel good. Some of it may be unhelpful or unkind, in which case you can draw a learning from it if you wish, or you can set that data completely aside as an outlier that doesn't concern you.

---

[26] I learned this from a brilliant now-out-of-print book: *Just Enough Research*, by Erika Hall, published by A Book Apart. If you ever come across a copy, buy it, whatever the cost.

The book you're holding in your hands only exists because after two years of writing and rewriting in private, I had all but given up on ever finishing a manuscript. On my fourth full rewrite, I decided to write the first three chapters as blog posts and share them on my website and mailing list. Feedback started to come in—some of it critical and constructive; some of it unqualifiedly cheering. I still and probably always will struggle with critical feedback even when it's well-intentioned due to my own funky mental and emotional wiring, but the momentum I felt from the cheers kept me going. That data told me there was an audience for this book, and here you are, reading it.

I forget this lesson often and try to remind myself routinely. If I notice my thinking starting to fractal and the anxiety kicking in, I ask myself: *What can I publish/launch/share right now that will yield some data to break the overthinking pattern in my head?* If you're anything like me, your "move fast and learn things" muscles will have to be found, exercised, and maintained in order to have any chance of competing with that big amazing brain of yours. It's absolutely and completely worth the effort.

WATCH OUT FOR OVERLY SPECIFIC OBJECTIVES

Sometimes, especially in implementation and execution areas of the business, you might find yourself writing objectives that are quite narrow. You can tell an objective is too narrow when you start to ideate key results and you realize that one key result is just a restatement of the objective with numbers added to it.

> Objective: Launch with no critical bugs.
> Key Result: Zero P1 bugs.

> Objective: Increase efficiency in customer support
> responses.
>   Key Result: Decrease time to initial response by
>   10% (from 10 min to 9 min).

Instead you can zoom your lens out by asking yourself: "Why is that important?" Sometimes your most important key results come from understanding your *why*, not just your *what*.

> Objective: Launch with no critical bugs to ensure
> strong media coverage from Day 1.
>   Key Result: Zero P1 bugs as launch.
>   Key Result: 25% of journalists on our wishlist
>   cover our product release favorably within
>   seven days of launch.
>   Key Result: 100% of media mentions about new
>   product launch mention our reliability as a
>   selling point.

See how much more impactful that second OKR set is in communicating what's really important?

Your objectives may be too narrow if you're having trouble getting them down to a manageable number. If you've got a long list of potential objectives, again try zooming out. Touch base with the themes that are important for you to create objectives around. If there's a lot of overlap between your candidate objectives, you may be being too detailed about implementation. Your strategic thinking may benefit from zooming out.

Also, if you find yourself putting a number in your objective, you may be creating a key result, not an objective. Creating an objective around a metric or anything that's going to be quantified, again, suggests that it's time to zoom out a level and identify a directional goal instead of a measurable goal. Of course, keep track of that quantifiable goal idea since it may become a key result.

You can always begin with an objective that breaks this rule and then test it by creating key results for it. If your key results provide clarity and alignment, then you can move forward with an objective that breaks the rules. But if you have an objective that is too specific or quantifiable and the resulting key results are basically activities, it may mean that you've written an objective that's too narrow and that would benefit from expanding to a broader lens.

WHAT IF YOUR WHY IS "BECAUSE WE'RE A BUSINESS AND HAVE TO MAKE MONEY"?

If a team is struggling to answer the question of why something matters, eventually someone's likely to half jokingly blurt out ". . . because we're a business, and we have to make money."

While that is true—businesses must make money—rarely is that a shared purpose that anyone outside of CEO, CFO, and the sales department get excited about. So even when you're ideating objectives in the revenue and finances arena, if you run into the dead end of "because we're a business and must make money" as the *only* potential purpose statement for an objective, a third line of questioning can get you back on the road.

- To whom is this most important?
- Why does it matter to them?

There might be some discussion here about internal stakeholders, external stakeholders, and often some disagreement about who is the most important constituency to center. But you can ask the team to think about who is ultimately going to determine whether this objective has been achieved. Whose point of view is most important? Centering that constituency clarifies the *why* clause so that you can best serve that constituency's needs.

Once a constituency is identified as the determiner of success for the objective, you can re-ask the *why* question from their point of view. "Why does this matter for our most important constituency?" The answer to that question may yield the fodder you need to get to a more inspired shared purpose.

TL^DR: STRATEGIST TAKEAWAYS

Create objectives quickly by:

- Gathering input.
- Narrowing the choices.
- Asking and answering two main questions:
  - What is most important to achieve in this goal cycle?
  - Why does that matter (and to whom, if necessary for clarity)?

8

Key results are the most challenging piece of the OKR process for most organizations to master. It is incredibly appealing to stay in plan-land—planning the activities you know or think you can control—instead of having the courage or creativity to identify actual key results—empirically measurable but aspirational outcomes you hope to influence but are beyond your control.

I have an uncomfortable truth for you: Innovation, transformation, and growth all happen from stepping out of that control zone and into the unknown. In the No-BS OKR model, key results are where you challenge yourself to courageously do just that.

Leaders asking their teams to implement OKRs often do so with visions of quantifiably improved performance by their teams, with crisp, clear charts and graphs in lovely dashboards that leaders can look at on a weekly basis to increase their confidence that they understand the progress of their business and where any risks lie.

In part, that's because those dashboards are big business. OKR specialty platforms exist in part to enable those dashboards. But

No-BS OKRs are about more than dashboards. Personally, rather than a perfectly instrumented, multiple-layers-of-localization dashboard that quantifies what is easy to measure instead of what is most important, I would like to see an organization with:

1. Company-level OKRs in a single slide.
2. A simple spreadsheet to track progress on the company-level OKRs.
3. Regular communication of those company OKRs and their status to the organization.
4. Open communication from leadership about wins and new knowledge, modeling the intellectual humility, curiosity, and courage they expect from their organization.

However, getting leadership to articulate key results—empirically measurable goals for progress or definitions of success—can be incredibly difficult. Too often when senior leadership sees measurable accountability as other people's responsibility and fails to model it themselves, team members lack the psychological safety needed to stick their necks out. Few corporate cultures create the conditions where people feel trusting, safe, and happy to suggest quantifiable goals that they are not confident they can achieve.

The truth is, when you're setting goals you're confident that you can achieve—or that are within your control—you're not setting goals, you're creating plans. Get comfortable with the idea that data is information, which is neutral, and not "good" or "bad." Encourage team members to identify measures

> **When you're setting goals you're confident you can achieve, you're not setting goals, you're creating plans.**

for their work that motivate them to pursue their goals even with the risk of non-achievement.

WHAT MAKES A GREAT KEY RESULT?

Great key results have a single clear, important metric or measure that is a focus of improvement. In other words, if there isn't a number in it, it probably isn't a key result.

As mentioned earlier, I coach a textbook key result (explained in detail later):

[Increase/decrease/improve] [a metric] by [X%] from [Y] to [Z]

That formula makes it nearly impossible to put forth a key result that isn't quantifiable.

No-BS key results are complete on their face. They specifically include the direction of change (increase, decrease, or improve), the exact metric or measure, the degree of change you expect, and a clear identification of the start value and finish value.

No-BS key results are either frequently measured leading indicators (a progress metric) or one of your most important outcomes (typically lagging and sometimes binary measures).

No-BS key results leverage verbs that go in a direction: increase, decrease, improve, etc. Make sure your key results measure progress in a direction, not describe an activity. When a key result revolves around activity verbs (like implement, launch, create, draft, build, write, develop, or any number of others), it deserves scrutiny.

No-BS key results are empirically measurable and exclude subjective estimates of progress or activity completion. They give clear

No-BS key results are empirically measurable and exclude subjective estimates of progress.

data to support decisions about performance during the goal cycle and a clear understanding of the shared outcome you're aiming to achieve.

No-BS key results focus on one metric each. Multiple metrics in a key result can make it mathematically impossible to quantify success. For example, consider this candidate key result:

> Achieve an average product review rating of five
> stars during the two weeks after Product X's
> launch, with a customer feedback survey result of
> 6.7 or better.

How would one quantify progress if the launch achieves an average rating of five stars but not until the third week after Product X's launch? Or what if the launch achieves a customer feedback survey result of 6.8, and an average rating of 4.5 stars. Is that a success? This example would benefit from being broken into two key results so that it's precisely clear what's being measured in each.

Even split into two, that example gives another teaching opportunity. No-BS key results include a specific target, not a target range. So rather than having a key result that says:

> Achieve a customer feedback survey result of 6.7
> or better.

A stronger key result has one precise target:

> Achieve a customer feedback survey result of 6.8.

As you can see, the first one is fuzzy about the goal. Which is considered success, 6.7 or better than 6.7? Just have 6.8 as the goal. If a higher result than that is achieved, so much the better.

The threshold I encourage for setting stretch key results is the answer to the question: "What do we hope to achieve if everything goes right?" That threshold yields a sufficiently challenging key result that encourages high performance but is still within the realm of possibility, which is important. Difficult goals that are not impossible yield strong performance.[27]

Take a look at this flawed key result.

> Improve customer support responsiveness by 10% by implementing team training.

You can't tell whether 10% is a lot or a little since there is no before and after metric stated. Additionally, including the tactic ("by implementing team training") is unnecessary. If what's important is improving customer support responsiveness, shouldn't teams and individuals have the freedom and flexibility to adjust their tactics to achieve the goal?

A stronger key result would be something like this.

> Improve customer support responsiveness by 10% (from 10 minutes to 9 minutes on average).

---

[27] Source: Locke, E. A., & Latham, G. P. (2006). "New Directions in Goal-Setting Theory," *Current Directions in Psychological Science*, doi.org/10.1111/j.1467-8721.2006.00449.x.

This makes it clear what's important and leaves implementors the flexibility to choose how to achieve that target.

"Creating goals and not achieving them is demotivating."

I hear the above a lot from prospects when I mention the importance of creating aspirational stretch goals.

While it is true that "nothing hinders the change process more than setting unrealistic and unachievable goals,"[28] when people set goals that they know they can achieve, statistically they tend to achieve at that level. This is fine in situations that call for incremental change; you can achieve performance that's a little better each time by maintaining this type of goal setting. This is also the preferable type of goal setting in an environment where it is not safe to fail—where there may be negative consequences for non-achievement.

But if it's necessary to achieve more than incremental change—if it's necessary to grow and expand and transform and innovate into the unknown—then by definition you are setting goals that you don't fully control the outcome of. In a psychologically safe and healthy environment, when teams set goals that are a stretch, this can be exciting and adventurous. OKR coaches frequently observe that teams tend to surprise themselves by performing beyond what they thought was possible.

---

[28]   Insight is borrowed from the field of health and well-being coaching but in my experience applies equally well in the workplace. *Coaching Psychology Manual*, p. 133.

Motivation science data says the same thing—you get your highest performance and a longer effort toward goal achievement when goals are set at a difficult level.[29] You want goals to be possible or realistic; you want them to be within the realm of possibility—if they're unobtainable, that can be demotivating. But if you set your goals at the threshold of challenging and still possible, that tends to inspire an optimum level of effort.

"If it's all winning and learning, where is the accountability?"

With the emphasis on safety to fail and on the stretch and learning focus of OKRs, you may be wondering: "What about the stuff that has to get done? Does this create an environment with zero accountability or consequences?"

OKRs are the place to clarify stretch aspirations that take you into uncertain territory: growth, innovation, transformation, and experimental terrain. Just because team members are safe to fail on OKRs, that doesn't mean they're not expected to make a good faith effort. Sitting out of or short-shrifting effort on an important OKR is a performance issue that should be recognized and addressed.

For stuff that has to get done, that's what mandatory goals and delivery plans with committed milestones are for. Those may be listed alongside OKRs, but they should always be clearly identified, so that people responsible for them are crystal clear about their accountability.

[29]   Locke, E. A., & Latham, G. P. (2006). "New Directions in Goal-Setting Theory," *Current Directions in Psychological Science*, doi.org/10.1111/j.1467-8721.2006.00449.x.

FOCUS ON THE KEY RESULTS THAT ARE MOST IMPORTANT

Conventional wisdom on key results is that teams should create four to six key results per objective. In actual practice, this makes teams feel like they must create an impressive number of key results to not appear lacking, which is not the mindset that you want. This is another place where I diverge from that standard best practice. Instead, I coach drafters to identify the key results that are ultimately most important and limit them to as few as possible. I would rather see one solid progress key result and one solid outcome key result for an objective than see four to six key results that are arbitrary targets for KPIs or that describe activity.

Traditional OKRs	No-BS OKRs
Create 4–6 key results per objective.	Create key results only for the most important/critical measures of progress and success, usually a minimum of one outcome goal and one progress goal.

When creating your key results, think about what information you'll need in your aspirational tracking dashboard to inform the decisions you'll make now and after goal-term end. But don't stop there. Key results are an opportunity to identify the aspirations that you dream of achieving. In your key results, you're communicating the quantifiable impact you want to have on the world around you and the ways that you want to create a different, improved future.

While I do ask teams to think about metrics and measures of importance, I also rely on broader and more aspirational questions. If you begin and end your questioning with metrics and measures, you'll tend to create key results based on what you currently measure. You may miss metrics that could be important. This is why—way back in Part 1—I encouraged you to notice the potentially measurable words in your strategic artifacts and Big Think. You might find as much (if not more) insight about what's most important to measure in those notes than by thinking hard about metrics and measures.

Now, let's look at how to think creatively about quantifying progress and impact.

THE THREE KEY RESULT TYPES

The three types of key results that are most transformative in organizations wired for change are: textbook, target-behavior, and baseline.

Textbook key results

The **textbook key result** (mentioned above) works best when you have an existing instrumented metric that requires improvement. These follow the formula:

[Increase/decrease/improve] [a metric] by [X%] from [Y] to [Z]

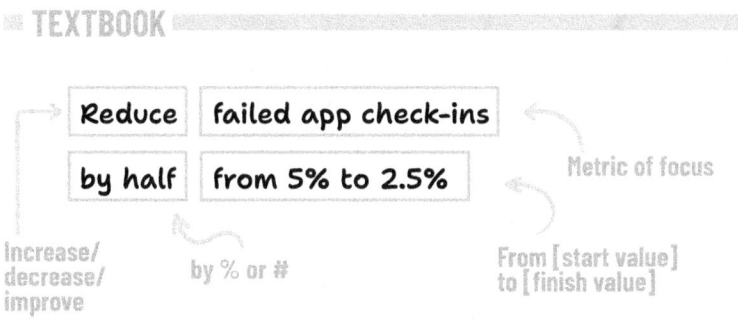

Target-behavior key results

The **target-behavior key result** (which I have also called in my trainings "behavioral," "observational," "noticing," or "low-fidelity" key results) fits when you don't have an existing metric but there is an observable behavior, spontaneous feedback, or other actions/effect that you notice happening as you pursue your work. These typically follow formulas like:

[Increase/decrease/improve] [a metric] by [X%] from [Y] to [Z]

[Increase/decrease/improve] the number of times per [cycle] we observe [phenomenon] by [X%] from [Y] to [Z]

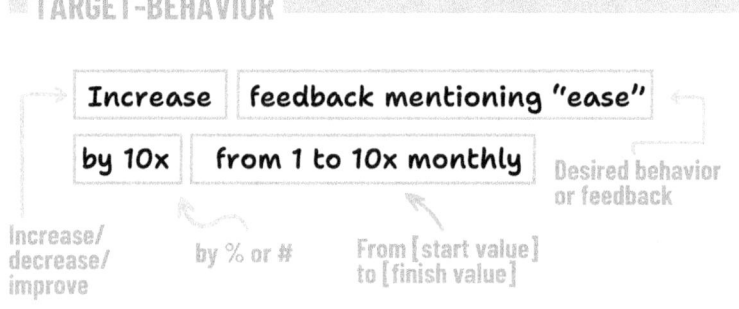

Baseline key result

Finally, the **baseline key result** introduces a new success metric to enable the creation of a textbook key result in future goal cycles. These are more general and follow a formula such as:

Build and instrument a model to measure [metric] and
baseline its [increase/decrease/improvement][30]

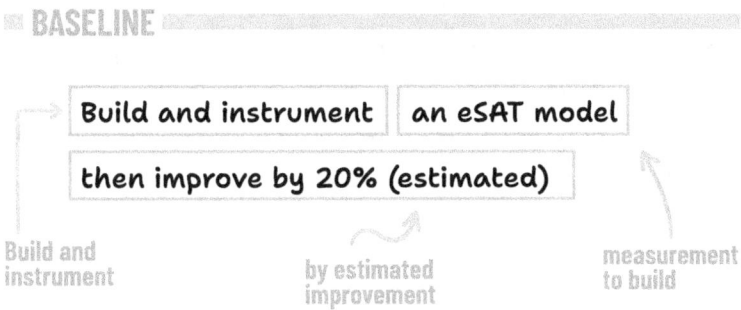

MORE ON THE TARGET-BEHAVIOR KEY RESULT

The target-behavior key result structure might be new to you, but it
can be incredibly transformative for organizations and individuals.

When a client is stumped on how they might quantify their progress or success, I ask them what they've been hearing or noticing.
Sometimes it's a quirk of the business that sparks curiosity or a surprise result that has been occurring without effort. You don't want
to ignore these things; instead, investigate to see if understanding
them is beneficial and should in fact be systematized and measured.
This stretches your thinking beyond the business metrics that live
in your dashboards today and forces you to consider the innovative
and experimental.

Here's an example from my own experience. Early in my practice at
Red Currant Collective, before we had much in the way of quantitative
client success or satisfaction data, I found it especially rewarding to

---

[30]   This is an exception to not including activities in KRs because the outcome is a
number (the baseline itself), not the activity of creating the baseline.

hear from workshop attendees: "That was a really good use of my time," "Can we do this again?" or some variation of "That was really easy," in a tone of surprise. Sometimes clients even used the word "fun" to describe their work with us. When I heard those things, I knew my work was on the right track; if I didn't hearing those things regularly, it made sense to re-evaluate my approach.

I started to play with developing a key result for my work to account for this.

> Increase positive spontaneous exclamations after workshops and classes by 3x (from 1 to 3 on average).

After we were routinely exceeding that key result, I created a new one:

> Increase the rate at which at-start detractors/ skeptics express some version of "That was a good use of time" or "Can we do that again?" by the end of the experience from 1 per workshop to 3 per workshop.

Another example from my own OKRs:

> Increase the rate at which clients spontaneously mention "ease" or "easy" during workshops or trainings from 50% of interactions on average to 1x per interaction.

This style of key result allows you to track the number of times a particular behavior happens (which may turn out to be an important

KPI as well as a key result) in an arena where you'd ordinarily be operating purely on a subjective sense of progress and success.

Is that perfect data? Would I bet my company on one of these key results? No. Have they provided improvement data, and ultimately, are they an important indicator of when my work is on or off track? Absolutely.

Could I use feedback surveys to achieve the same result? Perhaps. I did try this. Feedback surveys with predominantly high scores emphasized what was working—which let me know what not to change. When there was an outlier detractor here and there, upon analysis their displeasure usually had little to do with me and everything to do with their frustration with their own workplace or with innate characteristics of mine (gender, age, tattoos). So, feedback surveys often provided little useful direction for what or how I might improve.

On the other hand, the tracking of spontaneous utterances provided context. I learned to stop in the moment and maximize the encounter. Since the comments occurred in real time, tandem to my delivery, upon gentle further questioning they often yielded insight. Rather than an impersonal feedback survey where detractors felt free to say irrelevant or unhelpful things, the insights gathered after those quick utterances proved invaluable in terms of what was working and what could be improved. The utterance itself "pre-qualified" the feedback: the person cared enough to say something spontaneously. When one person said something, often others would chime in, providing deeper insights than if everyone is siloed off in their own feedback survey.

IMAGINING A BETTER OUTCOME

Another benefit of target-behavior key results is that when you write these, you're solidifying in your own mind what behavior or feedback lets you know if you're on track. That imagining makes the outcome you hope to achieve concrete instead of abstract—the questioning for this type of key result forces you to imagine what the world would look like when you've improved. This is one step beyond most people's natural thinking since many stop at the edge of their control.

Here's what this conversation looks like with a (sadly) large number of OKR workshop participants:

Client: "My work doesn't have an impact, I just have to do it."

Coach: "If you do your activity well, what becomes different in the world?"

Client: "I can't say; all I can do is do my activity, that's all that's in my control."

Coach: "But is mere completion of the activity the goal? Or should that activity result in some impact?"

Client: "All I can control is the completion of my activity."

Coach: "When you finish your activity and look around, what's changed in the world around you? Is anything different for customers or your colleagues or stakeholders? Is there feedback you'd like to hear? Is there behavior that will be observably different?"

Client: "When I finish my activity, there will be another activity for me to do."

It's like a mental block—which may exist for good reasons involving protective conditioning and possibly even trauma from the average workplace. However, a client in this mindset can't imagine an improved future—they're stuck in their present.[31]

However, when participants take the bait in the way these questions encourage, sometimes magic happens. An example: In a company I knew where transformation had become imperative to survival, leadership wrestled with their slow-moving, large enterprise culture. Team members had been conditioned for years that it wasn't safe to take risks; however, now, given the state of their industry, if they didn't take risks, their business risked failing. Creating a key result around culture improvement proved challenging one cycle. Employee survey feedback was muddled, with no way to tell potential innovators from disengaged team members actively resistant to change.

I asked: "What behavior will change when culture is improving in the ways you would like it to?"

Leadership participants shared thoughts like:

- People are willing to take more ownership of things and act with more independence.
- People feel safe to ask forgiveness not permission on basic decisions that are within their remit.

---

[31] OKR coaching tip: With a participant like this, if they're fully resistant to thinking in terms of outcomes they may influence but not control, I shift gears and ask them to identify their most important projects, and then we try similar questions about their projects—sometimes thinking about a specific project can make desired outcomes more tangible. Sometimes also, you can ask about pain points that could be resolved and focus more on pain relief than on growth and opportunity. In this case, I'm gentle and supportive; there are many roles in organizations where people lack the authority or autonomy to affect outcomes beyond completion of their work. People in such roles should be supported around that reality, not made to feel "less than" or like there is anything "wrong" with them because they're in that position. Their work may be critically important even if they lack autonomy or authority to pursue more than completion.

- Staff members ask a lot more questions during town halls; they're more willing to "hand raise and speak up" in that environment.

- Fewer questions arise about the boundaries of roles, possibly showing more confidence with a bias toward action.

- More spontaneous feedback occurs about enjoyment of cross-functional collaboration (e.g., "I love working with my engineering counterpart" instead of "I'm having tension with my cross-functional partner" or "I'm being excluded").

Even without a key result drafted, that's a pretty insightful wishlist right there. Knowing among themselves that the leadership team was in agreement on that shared vision impacted how they worked together and what expectations they set for their reports (and reinforced for each other).

Such a conversation can yield key results like:

- Increase number of staff questions asked during town hall meetings from 7 to 10 on average.

- Increase number of challenging questions asked by staff during town hall meetings from 0 to 1 per town hall on average.

- Increase instances of spontaneous feedback about enjoyment of cross-functional collaboration from 0 per quarter on average to 2 per month.

Or even some more "spicy" potential key results like:

- Increase rate at which a staff member demonstrates good judgment in decision-making while exceeding the boundaries of their role (asks forgiveness not permission) from zero times per quarter to 3 times per quarter on average per team.

- Increase rate at which staff challenge authority with a solid business case to back them up from once per quarter to 3 times per quarter on average per team.

Would you ever create a key result to fail?

One leadership team that I worked with wound up advancing a key result in their innovation and value proposition territory that I'll never forget. During discussion of the tough business environment they were facing, with a monumental modernization and innovation mission in a large, legacy organizational culture, the senior-most leader asked:

"What if we set a goal to fail more often?"

They needed to change behavior to embrace calculated and thoughtful risk-taking in an environment where—in the past—there was a pattern of consequences for failure to make "plan." The larger organizational culture could not confidently be said to be "safe to fail" within, but this leader knew that his organization was in an innovate-or-perish position. Even if failure was risky in the context of the larger organization, the risks of experimentation and failure were on par or lower than taking a safe path toward their own decline.

It breaks a few best practices in terms of verb choice, length, and multiple metrics, but here's what they came up with:

> Complete at least four projects we deem risky high-value experiments this year and achieve a 50% success rate (1/2 succeed, and 1/2 fail), with 100% of results documented and lessons learned celebrated.

When communicating the key result to the larger organization, it was an opportunity to be honest and transparent about the challenges facing the organization. Given the circumstances, it was a narrow line to walk: this was not a situation where anyone was safe since layoffs were possible, so the message could not purely be about safety to fail. The message was more: "We're all grown-ups, we know what situation we're in, and continuing what we're doing is not going to lead to success."

Most of the leaders I work with are driven, inspired, inspiring leaders of innovation and change—and that moment still stands out to me as an example of how to enable leaders to envision what's possible with truly courageous and intentional goal setting.

Having target-behavior key results right there in governing documents clearly communicates an expectation to the organization that you want to see these outcomes. Demonstrably. That means it must be safe to exhibit the behavior mentioned in the key result, which in some situations may require a significant cultural change not only among the staff but also among leadership.

The first objection to a key result like this is: "That's impossible to track." But it's not. Anything that is observable can be counted, even if it's with manual tick marks on a sticky note. Or, even better, with examples shared via your team's asynchronous communication platform, from which things can be tallied.

The second objection is: "But we can't control the outcome." Of course you can't. Remember: OKRs are your map to what improvement might look like. To explore that possibility, you have to step into territories you don't control. Anything beyond the direct activity of one person has uncontrollable variables (and even the direct activity of one person has an illusion but not reality of control). You don't control the outcome—but you may influence it. If you limit your goal setting to only what you control all the variables of, you're planning, not creating OKRs.

> **If you limit your goal setting to only what you control all the variables of, you're planning, not creating OKRs.**

Don't adopt a slew of target-behavior key results in one go, since they require manual tracking, but do experiment with one important such key result in your next goal set and see what you learn. If your experiment yields a favorable outcome, awesome. If not, that's still a worthwhile experiment. What did you learn?

A BONUS KEY RESULT TYPE: INDEX MEASURES

When you have a number of observable conditions, you can experiment with creating an index (a number derived from observations and used as an indicator or measure) of those multiple variables to fill the current gap in your data. Ask the question: "What information, data, or observations tell us we're on the right or wrong track?"

Each item that comes up may be one lever for progress or component of signal that you are headed in the right direction, and each can become one element of an index measure. Collect the index elements, weight them, and you've got a relevant experimental index measure you can test to see if it yields accurate signal on your progress and performance.

Like the S&P 500 Index in the stock market, an experimental index key result may be built by assembling a number of available contributing facts or quantifiable observations, weighting each, and calculating a single numerical "score" or index. Indexes may take some experimentation to validate, so don't trust that a new index experiment is instantly giving you good data. Over the course of a few of quarters, you can iterate and adjust the inputs and weighting until you're getting insightful information from the index calculation. What's the worst that can happen? After a couple quarters of low-labor experimentation, you may find that the index doesn't actually give you an indication of your progress. What's the best that can happen? The index you've devised may fill in an important gap in your measurement model, providing you input data that's important to your business and that you weren't able to quantify progress toward previously.

I recently coached a participant through creation of a "sustainability index" because she had observable conditions that could indicate improvement but not an actual sustainability measure itself. I asked her: "What data or information do you have that would signal that you're headed in the right direction on sustainability?" She replied with a number of criteria:

- "Replacing non-sustainable batteries in our devices with more sustainable power sources."
- "Transforming steps that require paper today into those that can/should be digitized."
- "Reducing reliance on vendors who operate non-sustainably; increase relationships with vendors who are responsive to our sustainability requests."
- "Introducing no new lithium-ion batteries into our eco-system."

We discussed which of those are most important. How should each be weighted? That then let us build a simple example index calculation table, shown below. Each contributing data point is weighted, has a start and finish value, and the attainment percentage can be tracked. At any stage, she can calculate her current baseline, and then set a target for improvement. Here's a peek at an example simple index calculation table to yield an experimental "sustainability score" for the scenario above, which can then power a key result like:

Improve (experimental) Sustainability Score by 27 points, from 43% to 70%

Example Index Calculation Table

Contributing Factor	Weight	Progress Value	Attainment Percent	Goal
Number of devices with lithium ion batteries removed from circulation	25%	1,582	20%	8,000
Number of steps in the staff service rhythm that require paper that we've eliminated	25%	0	0%	10
No new lithium ion batteries introduced into our ecosystem (1=True; 2=False)	25%	1	100%	1
Increase number of partners signed to our sustainability practices requirements	25%	27	54%	50
		Current Score:	43.5%	

An index like this may take experimentation to yield reliable and useful insight. Is it a perfect formula to bet your entire business on? Probably not. But in situations where teams say over and over, "We really need to measure X, but we can't," experimenting with an index measure can be better than nothing—and can ultimately lead to an instrumented business metric once the model is proven through experimentation.

Again, you may not be in control of the outcome of key results of this type but having them written can do a few important things.

1. They give you important clarity you may not have previously had about how you might best pursue your work.

2. They also enable you to test the importance of a potential measure. If you find target-behavior or index key results valuable, it may ultimately be worth building an actual instrumented measurement model to measure and baseline your new metric.

TL^DR: STRATEGIST TAKEAWAYS

*   No-BS OKRs are about more than pretty dashboards; they facilitate honest conversations about the present truths of performance, and are more concerned with doing better than looking good.

*   Key results may represent empirically measurable outcomes (lagging or binary measures) or progress metrics (leading indicators).

*   Limit key results to what's most important, ideally at least one progress and one outcome key result per objective; and rarely more than four per objective.

*   The main types of key results to consider when creating No-BS OKRs are textbook, target-behavior, baseline, and index key results.

*   Stretch key results should be challenging yet possible, encouraging high performance without being demotivating.

9

CREATING NO-BS KEY RESULTS

Now it's time to get into the business of creating key results. But no fear—you're not starting with a clean sheet of paper since you've done so much work already.

You've already done important thinking about potential key results—when you reviewed your strategic inputs and did your Big Think, you may have identified one or more words that point to measurability (or something that could be quantified as a potential progress or success measure).

Decide how long you want to spend on key result creation and set a timer. I recommend not more than one to two hours for getting to finished key results for all of your objectives. You may divide the work into two smaller working sessions: the first half for ideation, and the second half a day or so later for focusing and finalizing.

EXERCISE: KEY RESULTS IDEATION

Step 1: Create rough-draft key results

Pull up your One-Sheet and Big Think output and look back at the words that you circled when you reviewed it. These yield insight into what your key results might be. Before you try to write goals in the form of finished key results, narrow down your focus to what's most important and useful to measure by writing rough-draft key results.

For each of your already written objectives, one at a time, review all of your ideation so far, then ask and answer the following questions and create rough draft key results quickly.

- "What outcomes are most important for us to achieve in this goal cycle?"
- "How will we know empirically that we're making progress?"

Don't try to finish them yet. Just get your general idea on the page. At this stage they may have lots of question marks and blanks. That's okay!

Step 2: Focus and refine the rough drafts

Review your key result drafts and prioritize them. Which two to four key result ideas per objective are most important for this goal cycle?

Step 3: Edit the drafts

For each of your keepers, take a moment to write a key result draft that is as close to final as possible. Try for 2–4 key results per objective, ideally including at least one important outcome and a leading indicator or progress key result for any critical outcomes you need progress data on that's measured more frequently.

Why does this work? Aligning on empirically measurable progress and outcome key results keep you aligned on your most important outcomes and on quantifiable progress, not attached to activities you planned that may not be working.

Let a day or so go by before moving on to the next exercise if possible, so that you can sleep on the drafts you've created and see if any important additional insights come to mind before doing the refining and finishing step.

"WHAT IF I DON'T HAVE ANY METRICS TODAY?"

If you don't have metrics available as a starting place, you have a few options.

One, you could build or baseline a new metric to start out. In my brain, this style of key result has a number (the baseline) as an outcome, so it's an empirically measurable key result even though it doesn't follow the textbook formula. An example: "Build and instrument a model to quantify a sustainability index (then improve our SI by an estimated 10% quarter over quarter)."

Two, you could consider survey or other feedback data that's available (or can be implemented). This approach is a frequent "go to" for organizations to quantify the qualitative, but a couple of watch-outs:

1. Surveys must be well-designed to yield conclusive data instead of data of uncertain quality.
2. Many organizations and people tend to be over-surveyed. So while a survey may be the right choice in a given situation, surveys should not be defaulted to in all situations.

Three, you could consider target-behavior key results. These are the most underrated key result type I teach, and they can be powerful for achieving change or transformation. This style of key result usually must be manually tracked, so you don't want to create more than one or two in a given goal cycle, but that one or two can make a huge impact. An example: "Increase the number of times cross-functional partners comment on our collaboration skills from zero (0) to 4x per quarter, average." If you instantly object: "But I don't control that!" remember: you create key results you aim to influence, not that you control. If you control the outcome, you're making a plan, not creating a stretch-only key result.

EXERCISE: KEY RESULTS FOCUSING AND FINALIZING

All right, now that you've had a mental break, it's time to dive back in. From above, you will have draft key results and ideas about potential territories of interest but you may have reached a block around what they can and can't measure today. That's where important key results die, so let's not let that happen. Take about 20 to 30 minutes to walk through the following key result refinement steps.

Step 1: Are they textbook key results?

When you look at your ideas or drafts, first try to evolve them into textbook key results.

[Increase/decrease/improve] [a metric] by [X%] from [Y] to [Z]

Step 2: Are they baseline key results?

For the ones that do not fit that format, are they important enough to create a measurement model for? Is this a metric that when you get back together next time, you're going to wish you had a baseline on to improve on? If so, consider a baseline key result:

> Build and instrument a model to measure [metric]
> and baseline its [increase/decrease/improvement]

Step 3: Are they target-behavior key results?

For the remainder, are you trying to achieve some sort of behavior change or observable phenomenon that isn't a traditional metric? Can you develop an target-behavior key result through observation and tallying?

> [Increase/decrease/improve] the rate at which we hear
> [feedback] by [X%] from [Y] to [Z]

> [Increase/decrease/improve] the number of times
> per [cycle] we observe [phenomenon]
> by [X%] from [Y] to [Z]

Step 4: Are they index?

Finally, are there a few where the metric merits building an experimental index to quantify multiple "signals" of potential improvement (or risk)? These can be written in the same form as textbook key results, but imply the need for the compilation of data from several indicators.

It can take some creative thinking about what might be possible to land on for finished key results. When you're creating key results for measures that aren't currently instrumented, you do have to work a little harder.[32]

Even still, you might just end that 30 minutes with finished drafts of your key results.[33]

Why don't OKR coaches just give clients the answer key?

Once in a while, especially in more measurement-rich scenarios (at the company level, or in sales and marketing, for example) and I'm coaching key result creation in an OKR workshop, when it's all said and done, the team sits back, looks at the list—which may be fairly obvious in retrospect—and asks:

"Why did we do all that work to get to this set of goals? This is so obvious. Couldn't you have told us this is where we'd wind up?"

The key phrase there is "in retrospect."

If the key results were obvious enough to have been predicted from the beginning, they'd have been the first thing out of peoples' mouths when they started key result ideation. And yes, there are definitely patterns to the metrics and measures that organizations wind up identifying. But imagine I give you the answer key to a multiple-choice *chemistry* exam, and you sit down and mark those answers on an *anthropology* exam. Is there a chance my answer key would yield right answers for you? Randomly, perhaps. Are you likely to pass your exam? Probably not. And did you learn anything about anthropology? Not a thing.

---

[32]   Another read I always keep within arm's length in the event I want to nerd out is the book *How to Measure Anything, Finding the Value of "Intangibles" in Business*, by Douglas W. Hubbard (2014).

[33]   . . . and if you haven't, it's okay to struggle with efforts to create OKRs. But I never want you to *suffer* with efforts to create OKRs. If you're stumped, drop me a message at hello@redcurrantco.com and I'll point you toward additional resources or share a tip if I have one.

It's a relatively small investment of time to "do your homework" and your own studying for your exam; and it yields a far better long-term outcome than if I just show you a possible answer key.

TL^DR : STRATEGIST TAKEAWAYS

- Key result refinement starts with prioritization. Only do the labor of finishing key results that you will actually work to achieve. Don't write a finished key result for every idea you identify. Prioritize them down to only the measurement territories that you must include goals for this cycle.

- Set a time limit for key result refinement to maintain your focus and efficiency.

- Use creative thinking to develop measures for key results that aren't currently instrumented. If you don't have data to measure with today, get creative, and consider an observational key result that is manually tracked, creating an index key result by assembling multiple data points into an index, or a baseline key result.

- Aim for 2–4 finished key results per objective in most cases—ideally, a mix of textbook and target-behavior key results, with a few baseline or index key results to improve your data availability and quality in future quarters.

- Refine key result ideas into finished key results, ensuring they are powerful and useful.

10

KEY RESULT MISTAKES AND PITFALLS

There is a three-way tie for the biggest mistakes I see in key results: creating key results that aren't measurable; creating too many key results; and not creating enough leading indicator (or "progress") key results. The first two are tightly woven together.

THE "NOT MEASURABLE" MISTAKE

OKR experts don't agree on everything, but one thing most agree on is that what makes a key result a key result is that it is empirically—or in traditional OKR terms "objectively"—measurable. Every expert has a different standard of rigor around what they mean by "objectively," but nearly all coaches and sources agree that key results should be about measurable outcomes, not activities.

The best signal that a key result is measurable is if there is a number in it. If some of your draft key results don't contain a number, you're not alone. I see a lot of key results from clients both at the candidate and finished stage that have no numbers in them. If a key result doesn't have a number in it, I'm hard-pressed to understand how it's empirically measurable.[34]

The best signal that a key result is measurable is if there is a number in it.

But a number does not an empirically measurable key result instantly make. Many key result candidates have numbers indicating either subjective estimations of percentage complete or quantifications of activity.

In the case of a key result like, "*Complete 30% of the modernization-backlog roadmap items,*" the question becomes, by what method are you calculating that 30%?

If this team has a way to empirically assess their percentage complete, then this may be a finished key result if the starting and finishing values are included, for example if the team tracks the number and progress of roadmap items and can calculate their percentage complete. But still ask the questions: Is completing those roadmap items what's most important? Or does completing those roadmap items lead to some outcome that—if you aligned on what it is—might inform the decisions you make? Is the activity what's most important? Or is there a larger outcome that the activity should achieve? If an outcome is important, the key result should be about that, not the activity.

That brings us to a second type of key result candidate that also deserves scrutiny. Often teams will write key results quantifying activity and consider that empirically measurable.

---

[34]   *Measure What Matters* includes dates as a way of making a key result measurable, but even dates have numbers in them!

Migrate 27 of 100 legacy systems to our new
modern infrastructure platform.

The verb gives this one away: "migrate" focuses on activity, not the change from a start value to a finish value. What this candidate key result does is similar to the one above. It quantifies the number of times you plan to do something; in other words, it quantifies activity. Candidate key results like this should get the same scrutiny mentioned above. Is doing the thing a certain number of times what is important? Or is generating some quantifiable outcome or impact what's most important? The answer determines whether quantifying impact yields a worthwhile key result or whether the team should quantify the impact instead of activity.

The number test can usually determine if something is not a key result. If you need a backup test, you can also look at the words and ask: What verbs are featured in this key result? If you see verbs like increase, decrease, improve, or reduce, those verbs signal quantification and measurement. If the primary verbs in a key result candidate are verbs like create, implement, pilot, launch, build, release, prototype, or design, those are an indicator that—unless you see a directional adjective somewhere else in there—the key result is about activity not impact.

> **If you see verbs like increase, decrease, improve, or reduce, those verbs signal quantification and measurement.**

Q: Why should key results be measurable outcomes? Why not just plan my activities?

A: If you're starting with no planning at all, then you may benefit from planning your activities. Even planning activities gives greater clarity and focus than no goal at all. But with No-BS OKRs, since the focus is on achieving change and impact, what's most important is not what you plan to do, it's what you aim to achieve and what you learn in the process. If you were to run an activity-based key results experiment, what you will likely find is:

- Circumstances change, so what you planned to do may become outdated and your *how* may need to evolve.

- You may complete what you plan to do and still not achieve what you needed to.

- You may have been so busy doing what you planned that you missed noticing new growth or maximization opportunities that presented themselves.

- A host of cognitive biases may have kept you or your team pursuing your planned activities when objective data would have indicated were taking you in the wrong direction.

- You may find yourself very busy with no idea whether you're making progress or succeeding, or any number of other difficulties may arise.

- If so, you might in the next cycle be motivated to try creating key results around what you hope your activity achieves in terms of quantifiable impacts, instead of around the activity itself.

THE "TOO MANY" MISTAKE

The other major mistake I see in OKR creation is identifying too many key results. Sometimes it's literally too many: I've seen key result lists for a single objective numbering in the double digits. At that point, it's a laundry list, usually of activities or projects that need to be completed or the various KPIs to measure but not meaningful impacts or outcomes. Sometimes, there may be a relatively reasonable number of items listed as key results, but if it's five or six bullets of quantified activity and no goals that articulate outcomes, then the team may still not be aligned. They've got their checklist, but no waypoint to aim for together to inform shared decision making as they complete those activities.

When are OKRs best used?

One of the biggest issues organizations have when implementing OKRs is that a methodology meant to yield focus on what's most important instead may yield a huge volume of goals, not all of them actually meriting an OKR.

Distinguish between delivery workloads where mere completion is success (which do not require OKRs) and areas of the business you need to improve, grow, transform, or innovate: those areas of the business call for OKRs.

Making this distinction limits the volume of OKRs to a focused, clear number of most important change efforts.

Operational improvements to:

- Milestone/roadmap items.
- Run-the-business tasks.
- Sustainability.

THE OKR ZONE*

Growth, transformation, innovation, and operational improvement themes and initiatives

These benefit from OKRs to **clarify quantifiable improvement.**

These benefit from OKRs for **how you'll quantify progress and success.**

***What's Important:**

- Achieving a quantifiable outcome.
- Clarity mechanism(s) needed.
- Objectives and key results.
- Delivery planning.

OKRs are not required for:

- Milestone/roadmap items.
- Run-the-business tasks.
- Maintenance tasks.
- KPIs you're "watching"/maintaining but not prioritizing for improvement.

These benefit from delivery planning to clarify what must happen by when.

Much of the work of an organization can be characterized as "business as usual" or, as I prefer, "run-the-business."[35] The most

---

[35] Different businesses have different names for this type of work, if it's identified at all. I've heard: business as usual (BAU), run the business (RTB), and maintenance. Here, we're using "run-the-business" because I think, of the choices, that pays the most respect to the incredibly important work that runs in the background of any business to keep the lights on, payroll paid on time, accounts receivable collected regularly, and all the other critical business systems running. These workloads might not be as glamorous or high-profile as your OKR-aligned initiatives, but without your run-the-business, you don't have a business.

important thing about run-the-business work is that it is completed. These are the activities of your business that keep the lights on, keep the bills paid, and run in the background in a steady state or maintenance mode. Run-the-business activities don't require objectives and key results because they're steady-state activities. They're not activities you're going to change, innovate, or transform, and they may be planned as delivery workloads.

Now, if you have a run-the-business activity that requires improvement—let's say, an inefficient legacy process or a point of major friction that you've been avoiding fixing for some time—that may be the subject of a key result. But one of the common causes of key result overload is that an organization creates, or tries to create, key results for every activity in their business.

I emphasize with clients that while every person is important, not every task is important enough to create an OKR for. Your run-the-business and steady-state maintenance mode activities can be planned through your work planning systems; they don't require OKRs. Drawing that line reduces the volume of your potential OKRs significantly in most organizations and keeps the OKRs much more focused.

"Can I change my key result mid-cycle if I fall behind?"

Early in my OKR practice, I worked with teams and organizations where their OKRs were a constantly moving target. If something went sideways, the key result might be adjusted down, for example, to make the numbers look better. (Sadly, I also saw this later in my OKR practice, even in supposedly savvy OKR environments.)

This was problematic.

When you encounter a challenge or setback, if you adjust your target to make your performance look better, you miss the opportunity to discuss what went wrong and what you could do differently the next time.

Not achieving your key results is a feature, not a bug. In fact, it's one of the most important features of OKRs: setting an ambitious goal, working hard to achieve it, falling short, and then asking and answering the questions:

- Despite the failure, did anything work that you can learn from?
- What obstacles got in your way?
- What can you learn from them?
- What can you do better next time?

Asking those questions is the only way that, in a subsequent goal cycle, you can hit that goal out of the park.

So don't sell your performance short. If you don't hit a key result, leave it in the red and accept the discomfort of telling the truth. (It gets way easier the more you do it, trust me.) With practice, it becomes rewarding to tell the truth of what happened, receive support to right the course in the future, or make a joint decision to move on from a key result that's sending you in the wrong direction. In mature OKR organizations, the attainment distribution I aim for is somewhere around:

- 30% (or less) Green
- 40% Amber
- 30% Red

If all your key results are landing in the green, you're missing opportunities to stretch and improve.

LEADING INDICATORS ARE EARLY OPPORTUNITY AND WARNING SIGNALS

Identifying empirically measurable key results is quite difficult for most people at first. Even harder, though, is identifying measurable leading indicators. Once folks do have an idea of their important measurable outcomes, if I ask them: "How—during the quarter—will you know that you're either on track or at risk on your critical outcomes?" the answer is almost always a lengthy silence followed by a shrug. People can think about what they'll do to try to achieve their outcomes, but quantifying progress empirically takes real creativity.

Lagging indicator

A downstream metric or measure that ultimately changes as a result of the activities you undertake toward achieving your outcome. Lagging indicators reflect results; they don't predict results.

Leading indicator

An upstream metric or measure that provides early signal about the progress of your activities. Leading indicators predict results and help guide actions to achieve desired outcomes. Because they're predictive and proactive, leading indicators enable you to make adjustments before final results are determined.

The most reliable way to break through the leading indicator block is to use the analogy of a pipeline for a sales team. In sales, there is typically one or more revenue targets as important outcomes. Then most sales teams maintain a "pipeline," which provides an understanding of the stages that an opportunity moves through, from first contact to finished sale and retention. Every pipeline is different, but a simple example for a sales team might be something like:

Maintain an average 20 qualified leads in nurture stage

Maintain $250,000 in pipeline at 75% confidence of closing

$25k monthly recurring revenue

Sales and marketing teams are usually accustomed to working with pipelines; other functions may not be. But any important outcome has preceding "signals." This is a more helpful way to think about it than steps, since steps tends to encourage activity thinking and you want to think about what signals you can observe or count to ensure you're aware of opportunities or risks that may affect your downstream or lagging outcomes. In marketing, the concept is described as a funnel. At the top is "awareness," then the person moves through a "consideration" phase; and at the bottom is "conversion" (often a purchase) and sometimes post-conversion retention. Goals can be created about any stage of the funnel.

An example:

- **Awareness:** Increase social media amplification (shares/mentions) by 4x, from 1x month to 1x week.
- **Consideration:** Increase email click-through rate on list emails by 2x, from 2% to 4%.
- **Conversion health:**
  - Increase average order value by 25%, from $100 to $125.
  - Increase conversion rate by 1.5x, from 2% to 2.3%.
- **Conversion outcome:** Increase monthly recurring revenue by $10K, from $30K to $40K/month.

To design your own, for any discipline, you can ask yourself:

1. What are your most important conversions?
2. Which conversions are so important that you must have leading data on them because you're subjecting yourself to unacceptable risk if you don't?
3. What important micro-conversions precede those high-risk conversions?
4. Which of those possible micro-conversions give you the strongest signal of progress or risk on your high-risk conversions?

The answers to Question 1 give you the metric for your outcome key results; the answers to Question 3 give you your important KPIs; and the answers to Questions 2 and 4 may inform your leading indicator or progress key results.

It usually takes a few quarters of experimentation to determine which leading indicators give you the best signal, so don't bet the farm on a leading indicator until you know it's reliable. But with some experimentation, those leading indicator key results can become some of your most important. They give you data to inform decisions that may have previously been made subjectively or based on opinion in too many cases. Organizations often rely heavily on subjective estimates of percentage complete, which can masquerade as key results to the untrained eye given that they have a number in them. These subjective estimates are susceptible to cognitive biases that affect accuracy. However, they also give you early warning if something is at risk or off pace or early signal of opportunity if something is ahead of pace. So they're worth the experimentation effort to develop.

WATERMELON METRICS AND THE PERCENTAGE COMPLETE PITFALL

I just mentioned the perils of estimating progress based on percent complete. I say *perils* because what often happens is that a team or person relying on an estimate of percent complete may provide on-track status reports all quarter, only to have the actual important end of quarter outcome land in the red. For example, an engineering leader may report that a new software feature is on track per their estimate of completion during the quarter—increasing from 30%, to 60%, and ultimately to 100%—only to find at the end of the quarter that the feature had seven P1 critical bugs, preventing its release.

Percentage complete is thought of by many to be an objective measure—and it does have a number in it!—but estimating progress subjectively is rife with cognitive bias. Your organization won't get meaningful data to base decisions on if relying on estimates of percentage complete as a metric.

I occasionally get to audit large systems of OKRs—hundreds of key results at a time. As I've said, in most organizations the largest key result error is results that aren't measurable. The next largest key result error is quantifying progress in terms of estimated percentage complete. You can spot these because while they have numbers in them, they do not have a clear, objective metric to measure.

They may be obvious activities instead of outcomes: "Implement the new travel and expense system." This may include a progress bar showing 30% of 100% completion. Or they may be more sneaky: "Improve employee engagement and satisfaction by 50%." Again, there might be a progress bar showing a percentage complete, which one would assume means the organization has a survey or other objective data source for employee engagement and satisfaction.

On further investigation, however, often what you'll find is that, behind the scenes, the "data" informing the progress bar on the key result is a person making a subjective guess at how much of the activity contributing to that metric's improvement is complete. "We've completed two of the three employee engagement projects we have planned for this quarter, so we'll call it 60% complete."

This is one of the reasons I'm such a stickler for including the "from . . . to" in key results; with a clear "from . . . to," it's easier to spot whether the math lines up.

If the progress of a potential key result is going to be quantified in terms of an estimate of completion, I'd argue that serious thought should be given to whether that item should move to the delivery plan and not be in the key results.

Subjective estimates of progress are problematic for all the reasons discussed in previous chapters, not the least of which is that estimating percentage complete reflects activity thinking, not outcome thinking, creating the risk of "watermelon metrics"[36]

I first heard the term *watermelon metric* in a strategic implementation with WorkBoard, a leading OKR software platform. You're dealing with a watermelon when all quarter you hear from your colleagues that an initiative is on track. You hear, "It's in the green, green, green," in all of the status updates. But then, at the end of the quarter, when an outcome is expected, suddenly that metric has switched to red and is off track or missed.

> **Watermelon metrics get their name because they are green on the outside and red on the inside.**

When a team estimates progress subjectively throughout the quarter even though the projected outcome is quantifiable, this leaves room for a host of cognitive biases to come into play. For example, optimism bias makes a person feel that even if they're behind they can surely catch up. The bias against sharing bad news makes people avoid the risks associated with it in hopes that they'll be able to turn the situation around. People don't mean to estimate progress inaccurately; by nature, most humans are just terrible estimators. So it is essential that your implementation layer be built with this in mind.

Watermelon scenario examples:

- Status updates from engineering that alternate between "We're on track, and anticipate an on-time delivery" and "We're a little behind, but still anticipate an on-time

---

[36] I've tried to track down the first usage of this term and have been unsuccessful. If anyone in OKR circles is aware of the true origin, I'd love to hear so I can give credit where due for this helpful concept.

delivery." When launch day comes, you get the bad news from the QA team: "The launch is nowhere near ready."

- Updates from HR that they're executing lots of activities designed to improve employee engagement; then the end of quarter employee engagement survey comes in and shows a decline in employee engagement.

- Sales reports that their pipeline targets are met—they have what they need in pipeline at the necessary confidence level—but at the end of the quarter you miss your revenue target because sales didn't close the deals.

As you may have guessed, watermelon metrics get their name because they are green on the outside and red on the inside. Those parts of your business that routinely turn up green on the outside and red on the inside are territories that will benefit most from leading indicator initiative key results.

TL^DR: STRATEGIST TAKEAWAYS

- Aim for key results that are empirically measurable and focused on outcome and progress measures, not activities.

- Watch out for the common pitfall of creating too many key results. One way to keep your number of key results reasonable is to distinguish between routine tasks that need milestones or mandatory goals and significant change, growth, or improvement efforts where a measurable outcome or progress is important that benefit from key results.

- Leading indicators are important, since they provide early signal about progress toward important outcomes. Unlike lagging indicators, which reflect results after the fact, leading indicators help predict outcomes and guide actions to achieve desired results. Identifying and using these indicators can significantly enhance the effectiveness of OKRs.

- A healthy distribution of OKR attainment in a mature OKR implementation is less than 30% in the green, 40ish% in the amber, and 30ish% in the red.

11

OKRS AT SCALE

f you are a solo practitioner or are only creating goals for yourself, you can skip this entire chapter. In that case, you're only concerned with one level of OKRs—your own—so a scaled or multi-level OKR implementation isn't necessary.

On the other hand, if you are in an organization with two or more levels of organizational structure and you're learning about OKRs, the topic of cascading OKRs is inevitably on your list of concerns.

One of the big selling points of OKRs is the idea of cascading, connecting, or localizing[37] them, to connect the dots between strategy and execution down through the multiple layers of the organization in a (theoretically) clear, aligned way. This can work, with important caveats; but not the way most people assume based on reading other sources.

---

[37]   "Cascading" comes from *Measure What Matters*; "connecting" is used in Nivens and Lamorte's *Objectives and Key Results*, and other sources including WorkBoard and my No-BS OKRs model use the term "localization."

BEYOND *MEASURE WHAT MATTERS*

I'm not sure exactly where the idea came from that OKRs can or should be "cascaded" or connected down through the organization layer by layer, from the top of the organization down to each individual, but that's the model that many prospects land in my inbox looking to implement. It may be because some of the examples in *Measure What Matters* are so tactical; I really can't say for certain. But there is one element of cascading advanced by *Measure What Matters* that we *do* need to leave behind.

In the *Measure What Matters* model, which I am still asked about in almost every OKR class I teach, the model of cascading upline key results down to become subordinate's objectives was advanced. Some clients are quite attached to this idea. But, since you have by now learned the specific definitions of objective and key result, you might see the inherent flaw with that approach. Key results are not objectives.

In theory, people like the cascading idea because it seems tidy and organized; in practice, taking this approach means that the cascaded key result, placed in someone's objective spot, almost always yields a checklist of to-do items, not empirically measurable key results. Taking this approach keeps teams from creating objectives and key results from the bottom up that align their domain's contribution to upline objectives, key results, or even objective themes.

The idea with conventional approaches to cascading (or connecting, or localizing) OKRs is that you can start with organizational OKRs at the company level or top of the organization and then those can be sequentially rolled down through the layers of the organization into the domain of each suborganization, subteam, and even person in some implementations. See the figure below for a simplified visualization of what this might look like in a large technology and product organization, similar to an org chart.

Example Simple Localization Mapping

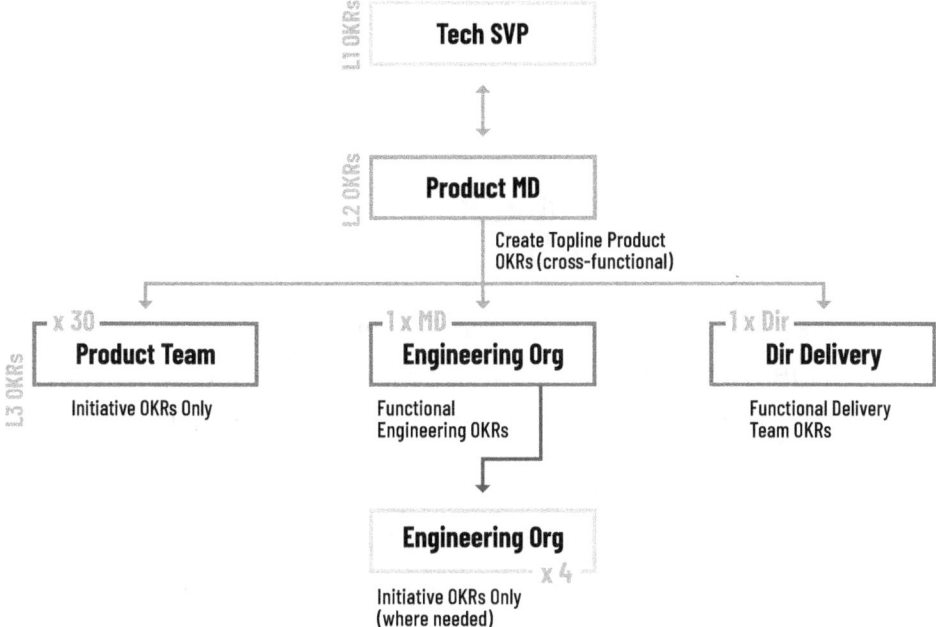

You can see that in the organization in the figure above, an OKR tree starts at Level 1 with the technology division all-up, then localizes down to Level 2 OKRs for product. The Level 1 and Level 2 OKRs can then be translated down (localized) to inform initiative OKRs for the product teams; functional engineering organization OKRs and delivery organization OKRs sit at Level 3+.[38]

The idea that OKRs can roll all the way down from the top of the organization to individuals sounds nice in theory—and a lot of organizations who implement OKRs are attracted to them for that promise.

In reality, localizing OKRs downward more than two or three layers is impractical at best and a time-consuming, frustrating

---

[38]   In an implementation like this, I think you can now start to visualize why I emphasize focusing on the smallest possible set of carefully selected OKRs so the total system of OKRs remains manageable.

disaster at worst, which inevitably yields lower and lower quality key results the deeper you go into the organization as the work gets more tactical. I've also seen that approach implemented as a method for micromanagement, which is not the best thing to be going for here.

A REAL-WORLD APPROACH TO LOCALIZATION AT SCALE

The alternative approach that I've been using working with OKRs at scale, without the downsides of conventional approaches to cascading and localizing, is to depart from a rigid layer by layer translation of OKRs in favor of recognizing that there's an art to the process that includes some flexibility.

Rather than by rote creating three to five objectives, then four to six key results at Level 1 and then the same for each Level 2 team, and then sequentially—layer by layer—cascading those OKRs deeper into the organization, the No-BS OKRs approach encourages creating fewer but more significant, carefully selected outcomes. This leaves room in your system for emphasis on goal setting among functional teams and colleagues, for cross-functional initiatives, and for any other important cross-functional priorities in the business.

When you have excellent, example-setting OKRs at the top of the organization, subteams can look up to understand what's most important across the organization and then ask themselves:

1. "Do any of the upline OKRs mathematically roll down to my organization, team, or initiative?"
2. "If not mathematically, which of the upline OKRs does my organization, team, or initiative align up to (and how)?"
3. In addition to those specific roll-downs and upward alignments:

a. "What else is important for my team to achieve, to further our upline OKRs?"
b. "Why does it matter?"
c. "How will we know we're successful (or making quantifiable progress)?"

That list of questions yields localized OKRs for that organization, team, or initiative, which can then be reviewed for alignment by the key upline and cross-functional stakeholders.

A No-BS OKR implementation might look something like the figure below. You can see there that:

Localizing OKRs in an Evolutionary Organization

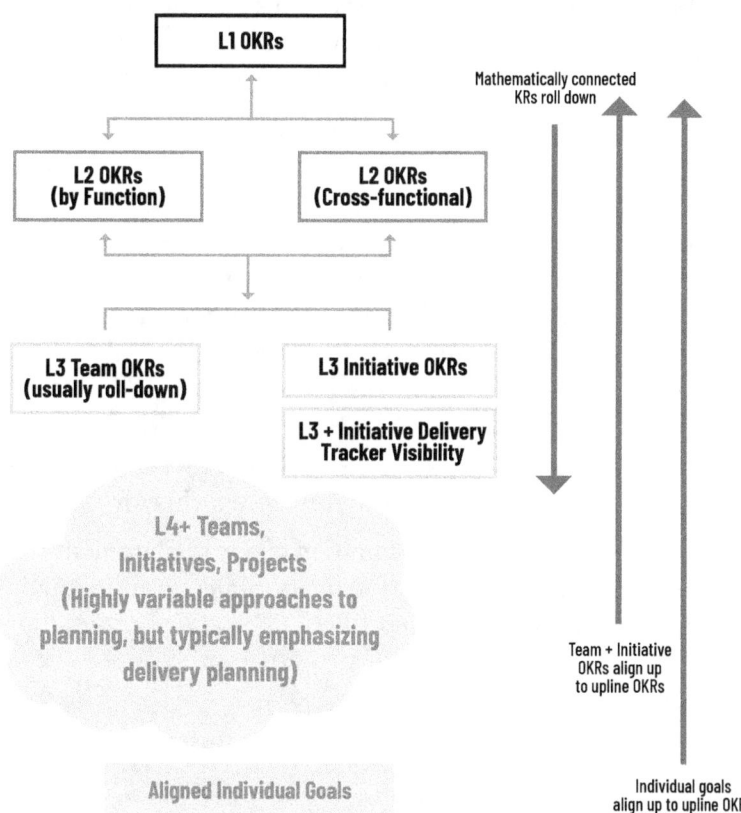

- When the Level 1 OKRs are set, key results may roll down to one or more Level 2 organizations (or cross-functional working groups).

- When the Level 2 OKRs are set, their key results will include both those rolled-down key results, as well as OKRs that the Level 2 team or leader creates for their domain that align up to support the Level 1 OKRs.

- If there is reason to localize further, at Level 3, I recommend rolling down *only* the key results from Level 1 or Level 2 where Level 3 makes an attributable, mathematic contribution. For example, if Level 1 has a total sales target and Level 2 breaks that into regions, Level 3 may break it up into subterritories. Level 3 is often where the initiatives that align up to achieve the Level 1 and Level 2 OKRs are agreed on, so at Level 3 it's common to have few actual mathematically connected rolled-down key results, and more milestones and initiatives identified.

- At Level 4+, often teams are fully in delivery mode. Workloads are planned in alignment with the upline OKRs and initiatives, and here teams may be fully focused on completion, not actual impact outcomes. OKRs can always be created in specific where alignment on outcomes and progress data is needed. But from an organizational OKR "tree" standpoint, they're often managed locally at this level and linked to from the larger organization's OKR tracking system rather than being tracked within the math of the central OKR tracking system for the simple reason that the math rarely actually rolls down this far.

- Aligned individual goals can then be set in alignment with the OKRs, initiatives, and delivery plans an individual is responsible for supporting.

This approach does a few things:

1. Organizations are able to spend more time achieving their OKRs rather than taking lengthy OKR creation and localization cycles (where each level must be complete before the next or have a formal alignment reconciliation) that may eat into implementation time.

2. The total number of OKRs in the system is kept to more manageable levels, since you don't have OKRs for the sake of having OKRs anywhere in the system; you have OKRs exactly where you need them, without redundancy or repetition.

3. With a smaller and more manageable number of total OKRs, it's more realistic for teams and individuals to be able to look up the levels for guidance (without having to dig through a lot of unrelated OKRs to find the handful that apply to their work).

4. Organizations that already have project management up and running avoid the data duplication and re-entry issue of OKRs living in both the project management system and the OKR system.

Implementing OKRs at scale using this method works very well as long as the Level 1 and Level 2 OKRs are high quality. If Level 1 and Level 2 have OKRs that are not modeling best practices, it may be advantageous to try to create full, best practice OKRs at Level 3 (by team and initiative) to be able to align up to the upline strategy for review with leadership to make sure that Level 3+ has clear expectations (even if they create them themselves).[39]

---

[39] This dynamic of substandard Level 1 and Level 2 OKRs, with Level 3 teams and people creating their own OKRs to create clarity for themselves is so common I call it the "L3 Conundrum." I'll share more about that dynamic and its risks later in this chapter.

Level 1: Company Level OKRs

Let's look at the characteristics of OKRs I observe at each level of the organization, starting with Level 1: usually, the company level. If you want to see an actual example of OKRs at each level of the organization, I've got you. You'll find an up to date best practice example on my blog at findrc.co/okr_localization.

At Level 1, you aim for a reasonable number of objectives and key results that reflect the truly most important outcomes and progress indicators of the organization and fit on a page, in a font size that is readable were you to hang them printed out on a cubicle wall or whiteboard next to your desk. The volume at the company level may be—for example—four objectives, each with two, three, or four key results. Much more than that, and you risk losing focus.

The company-level OKRs should align closely to the topline objective themes and topline measures for the year, if any are stated in upline strategic plans, annual operating plans, or budgets (or your Strategic One-Sheet).

Company-level key results are a blend of important outcome measures and quantifiable progress key results so that information during the goal cycle shows whether you are on or off track empirically.

Level 1 OKRs are lofty—like mini vision statements—and they span across the organization and therefore are often highly cross-functional. Key results at Level 1 typically include goals for the organization's topline measures and other critical company-level measures of progress and success.

Some large or global organizations may have a Level 1.5 that is "company-level-ish"—e.g., where Level 2 on their org chart is more like a company than a functional organization. For example, when Level 1 is global, Level 2 might be made up of regions that operate independently and to some degree like separate companies. Their

Level 2 could be considered Level 1.5; their Level 1.5 OKRs would look a lot like Level 1 or company-level OKRs.

Level 2: Functional organizations

Level 2 OKRs look a lot like Level 1 OKRs in most organizations. The volume is typically similar (3–5 objectives, each with 2–4 key results) but occasionally it's necessary to include one or more important milestones or mandatory goals because they are so important that leaders and key stakeholders want them visible alongside the OKRs at all times. That doesn't make those things OKRs: they are labeled specifically "milestone" or "mandatory" so there is no question what's what. You may see some key result roll-downs that apportion responsibility for a contribution to a Level 1 OKR to a suborganization or sometimes a major company-wide initiative. Functional organizations often receive a few of those roll downs, but that doesn't yield a complete set of OKRs for them. So, they then look up at the company OKRs to ask and answer the questions:

- "Are we directly responsible for a mathematical contribution to an upline key results?" (If so, the responsible portion rolls down.)
- "What outcomes or progress can we contribute to increase the likelihood that we'll achieve these company OKRs that aren't mathematical roll-downs?"

For those, you may identify roll-downs or roll-ups respectively, that support upline OKRs.

At Level 2, a suborganization's OKRs—including roll downs and created OKRs—should still fit on a single page. People within the organization's Level 2 can hear the Level 1 OKRs in the town hall meeting and then focus most of their effort on the Level 2 OKRs during the implementation phase.

If you sit in Level 2 of an organization that's highly executional, your OKRs on a page may look more like the "highly executional suborganizations and teams" style described below.

Level 2 OKRs may ultimately be highly cross-functional, but early in OKR implementations, organizations are often more focused on the ways that individual functional organizations contribute to or support the company OKRs at Level 2. Learning to create Level 2 OKRs is challenging for most; trying to do so cross-functionally off the bat proves too much for many. My best practice is to start with functional OKRs at Level 2, and then expand to include more cross-functional OKRs at Level 2 when the leaders start to spot the necessity for increased cross-functional alignment—and where, specifically, in the organization it's most required. When people self-identify: "We need increased cross-functional alignment on Project X and Initiative Z," then a cross-functional OKR creation team can be spun up for each and tasked with creating project/initiative OKRs together. Letting people learn where they need to increase collaboration and voice that need themselves is far more effective than trying to force cross-functional alignment from the beginning, which often makes little progress on breaking down silos or actually achieving improved alignment.

The Level 3 split

At Level 3, you see different OKR and delivery planning implementations based on the size of the organization. Let's look at enterprise implementations first, and then talk about what this may look like in smaller organizations.

Level 3 in the enterprise

Level 3 in an enterprise organization may be quite large and may have characteristics more like the outcome-aligned Level 2 teams described above. For example, some enterprises are still apportioning or rolling down mathematically-connected key results to Level 3. If there is a third level of connected math (think about the global, regional, subterritory example mentioned above), it may be necessary to localize actual OKRs to Level 3. But even in quite large organizations, that is surprisingly rare. (If you must localize to Level 3, be careful to maintain the definition of a key result and the distinction between key results and initiatives and their milestones.)

Organizations that must roll key results down more than two levels may benefit most from considering an OKR specialty platform—but not for the fully connected, cascaded approach advocated by conventional or early OKR practices. Instead, the complexity of managing math at more than two levels of attribution is a perfect job for software.

Even in the enterprise, some Level 3 teams will be more executional than outcome aligned. When working with highly executional teams, the Level 3 OKRs may begin to look more like what we're about to describe for small and mid-sized businesses: with a mix of objectives, some key results, some initiatives, and possibly even some milestones.

Highly executional organizations and teams

In small and mid-size businesses, if you're localizing OKRs to Level 3 at all, what's important for clarity at Level 3 may look different from the Level 1 and Level 2 OKRs described above. At Level 3 in small and mid-sized businesses and heavily executional teams, there may be few if any localized empirically measurable key results.

If the team is more executional and has less capacity, authority, or imperative to generate outcomes, they may have fewer (or no) theme-based objectives with more initiatives identified instead. For a team that has a large number of initiatives they're responsible for, I recommend—if possible—grouping them into coherent cohorts that share responsibility for similar outcomes. This, admittedly, may be messy, but even if the output is a bit messy, that reflects the reality that the team is juggling (and making that visible may be important for getting the team what they need to deliver).

The single page of OKRs for a heavily executional team might have one OKR focused on operational efficiency plus additional key results buckets as needed. Each key result bucket may have either an initiative objective or an objective based on grouping initiatives that share responsibility for the child key results.

Ideally, at every level, everyone in an executional organization can look at one sheet of paper to see the OKRs that their work aligns to. That single page may include objectives or initiatives, roll-down key results, and even critical-path milestones if important for clarity within the team and visibility with external stakeholders. It's also important to work hard to maintain the definition and integrity of the key result; key results must continue to be empirical measures of success. Always distinguish between key results, initiatives, and milestones so that words maintain their meanings and the aligned goal model remains coherent.

> **Always distinguish between key results, initiatives, and milestones so that words maintain their meanings and the aligned goal model remains coherent.**

"It's all semantics with you"—a quick sidebar on why words and meanings matter

When I wrote that last sentence of the prior paragraph I heard a former colleague's voice ringing through my head. One of his favorite ways to respond to my contributions (in my role as a strategy executive) was to wave his hand and say: "It's all semantics with you."

Some people think that an emphasis on consistent, coherent words and meanings is unnecessary. A lot of leaders, even after completing OKR onboarding and rolling their OKRs out to their team, still use the terms "goal," "objective," "key result," "milestone," and "initiative" interchangeably, as if there is no reason to distinguish between any of the above.

What does that lack of attention to semantics cause?

Massive, widespread confusion.

When leaders misuse important terms, three things can happen:

1. A certain cohort of reports hear the mistake and think: *If this isn't important enough for my leader to learn, why should I?* They then go right back to checklists and business as usual.

2. Their more diligent reports might hear the mistake and think: *Gosh, I thought [word] meant [definition], but I must have misunderstood. Now I have no idea what's expected of me.* They leave the interaction confused and frustrated.

3. Diligent reports who are less deferential to power or social signals might speak up and correct the leader (and often receive the "it's just semantics" dismissal in response, and—speaking from experience—is not great for morale).

It is okay for leaders to mix up these words and to make mistakes. We're all human, this stuff is not easy or uncomplicated. If it were, no one would need all these books and trainings. My insistence that certain, specific terms be defined carefully and used in line with their definition is not just semantics. After all, words having meaning is why we use words.

So leaders and OKR core team members, I beg you: At least please especially learn and consistently model the basic words and meanings of *objective* and *key result*. That's only two terms to learn. If you do, you'll model the most important part of OKRs so that everyone on your team can stretch to achieve their potential (and improve organizational performance while they're at it).

The Level 3 conundrum

High-quality Level 1 OKRs lead to high-quality Level 2 OKRs, since alert Level 1 leaders hold Level 2s accountable for creating coherent and quality OKRs. But sometimes, even with professional OKR coaching, Level 1 leaders might do a—shall we say—substandard job of creating OKRs.

I've broken down the myriad ways that OKR implementations go sideways at Level 1 and Level 2 in an online FAQ.[40] Unfortunately, the impact of poorly written or undisciplined OKRs at Level 1 and Level 2 can have unexpected results at Level 3.

Low-quality Level 1 OKRs tend to beget low-quality Level 2 OKRs. If quality is low at the top, there is little incentive for Level 2s to do the mental work of creating quality Level 2 OKRs, either because they don't want to make Level 1 look bad or they may lack the safety to identify empirically measurable goals lest they suffer negative consequences for non-achievement. This is another example

---

[40]   For more information, visit: findrc.co/okrfaqlevels.

of the importance of leaders walking the talk, since their reports will do as they do, not necessarily what they say.

With low-quality Level 1 and Level 2 OKRs, you'd expect to see low-quality Level 3 OKRs, right? Garbage-in-garbage-out goals, right?

Not always.

Certainly, in some organizations, Level 3 OKRs would then become a check-the-box exercise and may (if you're lucky) create some structure and clarity where there was absolutely none before.

But consistently, and more frequently, I see what I call the "Level 3 conundrum" emerge.

Rebelutionaries aren't only found in senior leadership. They are sprinkled throughout most organizations. When OKRs are introduced to an organizational culture, it's the Rebelutionaries whose eyes light up and ears perk up. They tend to feel a kindling of purpose catch fire. All of a sudden, an arbitrary and baffling organizational culture, with unclear and always moving expectations, in which those of us with certain personalities or cognitive wiring have felt confused, lost, and frustrated, is talking about the promise of clarity, focus, and alignment.

Hallelujah, these Rebelutionaries think. *Those OKRs can't happen fast enough, and how fast can I start using them myself?!* They attend the OKR socialization town hall with an atypical spring in their step, excited to finally learn what's most important and what makes their work matter.

Then up go the OKRs on a screen. Before the leader even starts talking, the familiar confusion kicks in.

> **When OKRs are introduced to an organizational culture, it's the Rebelutionaries whose eyes light up and ears perk up.**

- "I thought our objectives were about what's most important and why? Why are the objectives just a list of project names?"

- "I thought key results were empirically measurable outcomes. How are these key results if there are no numbers in them?"

- "This looks like someone took a list of what was already planned and then assigned success criteria to projects, instead of getting strategic about what's important and why it matters. How is this any different from what we've been doing?"

At that point some Rebelutionaries may recede back into the frustration and confusion that marked their pre-OKR existence in the organization. But others won't. That's where things get interesting (or problematic, depending on whether you're the Rebelutionary or their leadership).

Some of those Rebelutionaries are going to go back to their desks, pull out the company OKR playbook, and create high-quality objectives and key results for their work. They'll align them with their leaders—a Rebelutionary's leader may be impressed by the initiative they're taking by creating actual key results—and collaborators, and then get to work. The teams working with high-quality OKRs are going to have a little more pep in their collaborative step; they might feel more connected to the organization's success and more engaged with their work and collaborators.

The organization then gets to the end of the goal term. The Rebelutionary is excited to share their wins in the quarterly reset; they have a spark of hope that perhaps when their leadership sees how successful their OKR effort was, the practice will take hold and spread.

Skid to a halt. Instead, when senior leaders are not Rebelution-aries, it becomes painfully clear that they are not interested in learning or change. They're just interested in talking about change so that the rest of their organization will magically increase their production.

All too often senior leaders' eyes go right to the key results that were not fully achieved. Their questioning goes straight to activity ("did you do X, why didn't you finish Y, if you'd completed Z maybe you would have achieved the goal"). Rebelutionaries feel quashed; creativity goes out the window.

> **When senior leaders are not Rebelutionaries, it becomes painfully clear that they are not interested in learning or change.**

This, my friends, is why I call No-BS OKRs an anti-gaslighting mechanism.

The lower level Rebelutionary has created the conditions for sunlight to shine on some organizational incoherencies. It's a fact of life that leadership does not always welcome that.

So how is this a good outcome for you—a Rebelutionary?

If you're the Rebelutionary in this tale, you now can take stock of your OKRs, of your progress—of your wins and new knowledge—and know that there is nothing wrong with you. Gaslighting is only effective if you believe it and question or doubt yourself. You, my friend, have a paper trail that shows even your most vocal inner critic that you created OKRs in line with the organization's OKR playbook, aligned them with your leaders and collaborators, pursued them acquiring some wins and some new knowledge, and now are poised to make improvements for the next goal cycle.

If your organization doesn't celebrate that as a win that can be learned from and scaled, that is a them problem, not a you problem.

You can now use the skills you've developed to create a new OKR for yourself personally—around how to find a role in a workplace where you can do your best work and thrive.

If you're the leader in the story above, I would strongly encourage you not to roll out No-BS OKRs. Roll out any non-branded clarity and planning methodology in the world, including something similar to OKRs in every way except name, but just don't call it "OKRs." Because if you do, you're at a high risk of inviting a methodology into your organization that—if you don't do it coherently and model intellectual humility, learning, and the other key leader behaviors of No-BS OKRs—may result in your high-performers moving on to greener pastures when they suddenly OKR their way to immunity from organizational gaslighting.

OKRS IN LARGE AND DEEP ORGANIZATIONS

Okay. Back to localization at scale.

Even in very large organizations, there may be no need to localize a system of OKRs beyond Level 3. The matrixing of project teams, squads, pods, scrum teams, and other collaborative working groups below Level 3 may create an organizational reality that makes cascading further unwieldy and untenable.

The good news: The benefits of No-BS OKRs don't depend on an enterprise-wide adoption. The benefits of No-BS OKRs can be felt locally, among any working group, in any team, anywhere in the organization.

How then do the lower tiers of a deep organization benefit from clarity and alignment of objectives and key results if not through rote, structured, cascading?

What's worked for my clients is to shift to the more flexible model I mentioned in the beginning of this chapter as soon as you're no longer rolling down math-based key results. Instead of highly structured, layer-by-layer cascading approaches, in the No-BS OKR setting leaders model consistently high-quality objectives and key results at Level 1 and Level 2. Their organizations learn definitively what objectives and key results are (instead of only thinking about OKRs generically). Then, deeper in the organization, people can choose the right goal tool for the job.

- Need to better understand and agree on a shared purpose and direction?
    - Create an objective.
- Is it important to strive for a specific outcome?
    - Create one or more key results.
- Is this a territory where you've experienced watermelon metrics in the past, or where a watermelon scenario would be a large risk or setback?[41]
    - Create some experimental key results to see if you can iterate your way to leading indicators that accurately and empirically quantify progress.
- Does something just need to be done a certain number of times by a certain date?
    - Create a milestone.

This approach works well because working groups can align on and create only the specific goal types they need without the overhead of chasing goal types they don't. This keeps the top-down, centralized system of OKRs smaller and more manageable. It normalizes that while not everything needs an OKR, you can leverage the benefit of objectives and key results anywhere in the business.

---

[41] See Chapter 10 for a full description of the "watermelon metric" condition.

It also works well because if a team experiences a setback that shows they should have had more goal clarity, they've learned by doing that it's important to create that goal type for the next cycle. For example, if overly positive, subjective estimates of progress result in an important outcome not being achieved, the team learns the value of progress key results and may be more motivated to experiment with some next time.

"But isn't a quarter a long time for a team to learn something like this? What about the waste?"

What's happened here is not waste. What's happened here is learning that can lead to a reduction in waste as early as in the next goal cycle if it informs behavior change. The OKR system made that waste visible so that now you can reduce or address it.

It's a big shift to wrap your head around publicly making mistakes, but that's how you have any hope of eliminating that same mistake in the future. You can be told to develop leading indicator or progress key results for important lagging outcomes all day long, but you're never going to do it until you feel the pain of not doing it. At which point, you don't take convincing; you're already convinced.

One of my motorsports mentors, Dave Alexander, whose career as a crew chief extended to some of the highest levels of the global stage of the sport of motorcycle road racing, tells about how whenever he made a mistake when working on a bike, he'd call it out, loud and clear, for everyone in the garage to hear. Why?

"Because it's not a mistake until it leaves the garage," he'd answer.

He was normalizing the practice of recognizing mistakes before anyone gets hurt—learning from them instead of sweeping them under the mat and trying to hide them out of ego or embarrassment. In motorcycle road racing, Dave's lesson undoubtedly saves lives.

The best time to learn a lesson is before anybody gets hurt or before the waste occurs. But the second best time is right after someone gets hurt or the waste occurs. At that point you can ask yourself: "What happened? What can we do to avoid that in the future? What change must be made as a result?"

Bottom line: If you'd continued with business as usual without OKRs making the waste visible, you might be making that same mistake over, and over, and over.

"WHAT YOU'RE DESCRIBING SOUNDS LIKE CHAOS!"

Maybe so! You might ask: "How do we manage and track that chaos?"

My answer? You don't have to.

What's important for each level of leadership in an organization is that they:

- Understand what's expected of their team.
- Communicate what's expected in ways that set their reports up for success.
- Clear obstacles to progress and achievement and ensure that capacity and resources are available when possible to fuel progress.
- Have the information they need to be able to effectively report up and across on the team's progress, new knowledge, wins, blockers, and needs.

To achieve the above, you don't need a fully-connected tracking system for everything in the organization. What you need is:

1. A way to understand what's expected of the organization (provided by the upline OKRs).
2. A way to communicate what's expected to the organization (provided by the OKRs they create).
3. A way to understand the organization's progress and risks, by adopting meeting and communication practices that achieve exactly that.

The quality of the "data" reported deeper in the organization may be suspect, so spending thousands of dollars to make that data look good in a dashboard is a poor use of resources. Instead, invest in a working culture where people are confident and supported when they raise risks, needs, issues of concern, and other important truths, and where leaders actively work to clear obstacles and provide for team needs.

What's important deep in the organization is that implementation progresses as smoothly and efficiently as possible, and that risks, blockers, and gaps are raised, triaged, and addressed strategically. This means cultivating a focus on the truth, not on rote processes.

WHAT'S WRONG WITH TRADITIONAL APPROACHES TO CASCADING/LOCALIZING OKRS?

If you're skeptical about the alternative approach I've laid out, let's talk about the three main issues I see with attempting to localize OKRs in the traditionally concepted, fully connected way deep into an organization.

1. Fully cascading OKRs leads to a lack of focus

Models that cascade or localize OKRs down through the organization at large scale often generate enormous systems of objectives and key results. The sheer number of OKRs can make it overwhelming to extract clear direction. The purpose of OKRs often falls apart when organizations adopt a conventional large-scale cascading or localizing approach.

To see what I mean, think about a traditional best practice OKR implementation, in which at the company level the organization creates, say, four objectives, each having four to six key results. That yields somewhere around twenty key results for people in the organization to try to derive measurement and expectation clarity from.

Okay, so twenty doesn't sound like that much. Maybe employees could wrap their heads around that. But then things get complicated quickly, as cascading continues.

The senior leadership team at Level 2 looks at those twenty OKRs and asks themselves: "How does my slice of the organization support these OKRs?" They then each create their own three to five objectives, with four to six key results each (which are usually functional, thinking in their domain). If you have a five-person senior leadership team, the organization now has a total OKR scatter of 120 or so key results. This is a larger total volume than a No-BS approach would yield; cascading further creates a volume of goals only software can manage.

A methodology that was supposed to create focus, clarity, and alignment has created a system of goals that is untenable for anyone to wrap their heads around—not to mention what happens if someone then tries to factor in cross-functional OKRs. Straight cascading quickly becomes unwieldy in practice.

2. Key results "break" when teams lack authority

Another contributing factor to cascading OKRs failing is that key results may break at some level of the organization. Despite the argument that for any activity you must identify a desired outcome, the reality is that lower level teams often lack the authority and autonomy to define outcomes other than just delivering on assignments.

Most methodology guidance makes no distinction between OKRs at the various levels of the organization, but typically at Level 3 or Level 4, you're in the implementation layers. Some parts of the organization may have deeper strategic or leadership roles in which people have authority, autonomy, and an imperative to achieve outcomes. Other parts of the organization get tactical quickly, and the people may not.

Think about maintenance organizations, corporate functions like legal and finance, run-the-business teams, and even some engineering teams. It sells books and software to say every one of those people should be working toward outcomes, but the daily reality in many organizations is that a large number of roles can't. Yes, they can deliver on tickets or roadmap items faster, with fewer errors, but that doesn't take a full set of OKRs to communicate. One or two fairly obvious improvement key results may be all that's needed. When you reach this level of the organization, there are other ways people can identify the outcomes of their work and how their work aligns to the organization's strategic priorities. Let that team focus on quicker, high-quality delivery.

Teams write activity-based key results not because they're not trying hard enough nor thinking creatively enough but because what's most important for some types of work is that it gets done on time, with a reasonable level of quality.

This is normal. But when this reality is not deliberately addressed in OKR operations, it can be demoralizing for the lower level teams. Some get stuck at the identification of key results because they're responsible for doing a thing by a date, with no authority or autonomy to affect the outcome otherwise. This lack of OKR consistency is a standard feature in large cascading systems.

The frustrations that result are many, but the two most important are:

> **Teams write activity-based key results because what's most important for some types of work is that it gets done on time.**

1. Teams for whom it is easier to identify quantifiable outcomes or who are in more metrics-rich parts of the business may criticize their colleagues for being unable to identify quantifiable key results.

2. Teams for whom it is challenging (or not possible) to identify quantifiable outcomes for their work may suffer morale consequences.

Most organizations characterize their OKRs as what's "most important." If a team's work isn't reflected in OKRs, that may leave them on shaky ground on the critical question of: "Does my work matter?" Teams for whom there is little or no capacity to deliver growth, transformation, or innovation may feel marginalized.

If one purpose of OKRs is to establish how a person's labor supports the organization's strategic priorities, cascading may reveal that some work is treated as more important. If you're not careful and intentional, some roles and people will feel less important than others.

3. For motivation, rolling down a target is different than assigning a goal

Goals can move downwards through an organization in different ways. In control-oriented organizations, goals tend to be assigned down by senior leadership. I've often seen such leaders assign key results that describe activity. Not only do you have senior leadership avoiding the behavior that they're asking of the organization (key results for measurable outcomes), in some cases leaders transfer the labor of identifying the desired outcome to the team. Communicating clear expectations about outcomes is a core leader responsibility.[42] In addition, the assigning down of activity key results removes the potential for people and teams to design their own *how* based on their subject matter experience.

One of the most discouraging experiences I've had was in an organization where I sat in a Level 3 individual contributor role. We had company-level key results around growth and Level 2 key results around satisfaction measures to support customer retention. The CEO cascaded a Level 3 key result to me to launch a new educational program on a topic of their choice as an activity assignment. Since there were no success criteria identified, I asked what the actual outcome goals for the educational program were. The response was essentially: "Just do what you're told."

Even I, as an experienced OKR expert at that point, couldn't believe how disillusioning it felt to be assigned a task by a leader who could not tell me how success would be measured. To maintain my own motivation and sanity, I created my own outcome goals in

---

[42]   This is often positioned with good intentions as intended to give people and teams freedom to identify the outcomes that matter to them, but being asked to do so without clear direction can lead to wasted cycles spent on fruitless mind-reading or the creation of arbitrary outcomes.

the form of quantifiable key results. Two-thirds of the way into the quarter, after the bulk of my labor was spent developing the new educational program based on minimal and arbitrary direction, I was proud the program was nearly ready for beta review. Then, the leader's priorities shifted, and the program I'd worked so hard on was indefinitely shelved.

Did it matter to the organization? Not really. The degree of human labor waste even in well-run organizations is astounding. But did it matter to me, as a dedicated and hard-working employee? Frankly, it was one of the last straws for me with that role, which I left shortly thereafter.

For anyone who's worked in a startup, you're nodding along because this happens all the time. But in an organization working with OKRs, this should happen rarely, if at all. Instead, Level 1 and Level 2 key results should make clear what's expected in terms of outcomes that advance the organization's strategy. This allows non-arbitrary key results to be created at Level 3 around the contributing outcomes that labor provides. It allows Level 3+ teams to make decisions about what must be done, in line with their subject matter and organizational expertise.

Rather than assigning tasks, leaders should delegate the authority to subject matter experts to identify initiatives and key results that roll up to the Level 1 and Level 2 OKRs. This also provides for learning in the organization at large. Instead of focusing on a task assigned by senior leadership, the organization can focus on activity effectiveness. Instead of trying to please the boss, people can use their valuable brains to learn how to achieve what's most important.

That's not to say that goals can never be assigned. Motivation science shows that goals can be assigned successfully without inhibiting

> **Rather than assigning tasks, leaders should delegate authority to subject matter experts.**

motivation if communicated with a rationale.[43] In the example above, my leadership could have communicated that we needed a new educational program, and here's why (as a rationale).

Even if a leader doesn't communicate an expectation in the form of a key result or outcome goal, a rationale provides language that the recipient can then use to quantify outcomes. This meaning-making is important for motivation. Motivation can be intrinsic—coming from inside—or extrinsic—based on outside factors, like pleasing a leader. Communicating a task without rationale requires the recipient to read the leader's mind to have any hope for successful implementation—and not many job descriptions include mind reading.

When key results are rolled down to teams or people, the recipient can take that draft key result, consider it, and respond with assent if they agree with it, ask questions if the rationale is inadequate, and offer potential outcomes to ensure alignment if the outcomes aren't communicated with the assignment. In that way, a rolled-down goal should be considered an outstretched hand for a handshake that the recipient maintains agency to consent to or can communicate what they would need in order to consent and return the handshake.

---

[43]   Locke, E. A., and Latham, G. P. (1990). A Theory of Goal Setting and Task Performance. Prentice-Hall, Inc.. p. 708

TL^DR: STRATEGIST TAKEAWAYS

- Not every organization is going to localize OKRs: some may create OKRs at the top to increase clarity of strategic direction, stop there, and see high value.

- For organizations that do localize OKRs, best practices are to treat the Level 1 OKRs as highly cross-functional; Level 2 as a blend of functional OKRs by team and cross-functional initiative OKRs when present; and at Level 3 having localization be a blend of mathematical accountabilities rolled down as key results from Level 1/Level 2 and, initiatives and initiative OKRs "rolled up" to support the upline OKRs.

  - When an organization has strong Level 1 and Level 2 OKRs, it may not be necessary to localize OKRs further. With clarity about initiatives at Level 3, the next link in the chain may be individual goals that align to the organizational OKRs for each person in the organization, and team goals that roll up to L1 and L2.

- Be mindful that some teams and organizations may have a heavy run-the-business or maintenance burden, so may have few objectives or key results—but that doesn't mean their work isn't important. Avoid using language like: "OKRs represent our most important priorities," and be more careful with language to avoid alienating executional teams, with statements like: "OKRs address our current important transformation priorities."

- For clarity, remember is to use the key terms *objective* and *key result* coherently, consistently, correctly, and with intention.

PART 3

STRATEGY ACHIEVEMENT

This next part is a reference section. Everyone reading this book is going to be in a different place with regard to implementation, so there isn't one way to move forward that will apply to everyone. Apply what is relevant to your situation, and skip the parts that aren't.

- Most readers will benefit from **Chapter 12: "Identifying Initiatives"** and the "Personal OKRs distinguished from aligned individual goals" section at the end of **Chapter 13: "Aligned Individual Goals."**

- The rest of **Chapter 13: "Aligned Individual Goals"** is most applicable to organizational leaders and human resources professionals managing the intersection between strategy, group goal setting, and individual performance evaluation. That chapter gets quite technical, but it addresses the most common questions I'm asked by OKR implementers, so I felt it couldn't be omitted or given short shift.

- I would encourage you to read **Chapter 14: "Strategy Is Changing Behavior"**—it's short, but addresses how to avoid five ways I frequently see strategic goals fail unnecessarily. What's the point of setting goals if you don't do the hard work of changing behavior to achieve them?

- **Chapter 15: "Implementing OKRs"** continues the focus on behavior change in a more tactical way, giving an overview of a few other frequently asked questions around tracking, administrating, and resetting OKRs.

12

IDENTIFYING INITIATIVES

Now that you're clear on strategic direction, how to identify quantifiable progress, and a shared understanding of what success means, let's talk about what you're going to do. It's time for close examination of the implementation layer of the Connected Strategic Stack.

Project Plans/ Work Plans ⇢ Other Projects | Key Initiatives ⇠ **Most Important Major Initiatives**

Project and Initiative OKRs ⇠ ...which may have their own objectives and key results...

project plans | sprint plans

Individual Goals ⇠ ...and which may be supported by individual grwoth and development plans and goals.

INITIATIVES

When a method for achieving your OKRs is a workload important enough that failure will put your OKRs at risk, that's an initiative—the boots-on-the-ground method of making the key results happen.

(Everything else the organization does can be categorized as run-the-business activity.)

The term *initiative*[44] identifies a named body of work that will achieve one or more of your OKRs. Initiatives are the workloads that—ideally—align to the achievement of your upstream OKRs. They can also have sub-OKRs of their own that break out the work further.

Establishing topline key results leads to determining the activities in your business that will support them. Initiatives may be functional (the responsibility of one organization or team) or they may be cross-functional (a shared responsibility among multiple organizations or teams). Sometimes, a cross-functional initiative is so important, it sits at the top level of the organization. Think of a major new product release that the entire organization is mobilized to support. Sometimes, initiatives sit at an organization's Level 2 or come into the picture in large volume at Level 3 of OKR localization.

GETTING AND STAYING ON TRACK WITH INITIATIVE OKRS

When a subjective estimation of percentage complete doesn't give you the confidence you need that an initiative is on track (which it usually won't), it makes sense to create an initiative OKR that more precisely states the metrics for success.

In initiative key results, you can get creative in quantifying when you might be nearing a progress danger zone. If you suspect while implementing that progress or success is at risk, what are

---

[44]   Sometimes these are called "key initiatives"; we're choosing not to use this term to avoid confusion with key results. See Chapter 1 section about the implementation stack.

you observing that's giving you that sense? Are there any leading indicators or observable conditions (similar to the inquiry used for the target-behavior key results method) that you may be headed in a risky direction? Do you have any early detection warning signs?

These are all potential territories for initiative key results. Just like target-behavior key results mentioned earlier, this type of leading-indicator initiative key result can be some of the most transformative in the business.

Remember: An environment where team members are comfortable sharing early in the work that there might be trouble ahead is a good thing. It will enable you to access additional resources when needed. You'll be able to recruit executive support for clearing blockers. This is how OKRs become a way for organizations to get more comfortable with empirical truth.

> **An environment where team members are comfortable sharing that there might be trouble ahead is a good thing.**

So, leaders must commit to the practice of being calm and responsive, rather than reactive, to troubling initiative status reports. A leader's job in the face of such a report is to calmly ask the question: "*What do you need to get this back on track?*" and then work to deliver on the team's needs. A leader's job when any key result is in the red is not to seagull in to fix or evaluate or judge the work in progress and assign blame. Reactions like that are directly counter to the accountability and ownership that you're trying to create for your team.

Instead, use the moment as an opportunity to build trust and confidence that speaking up is a net positive. Be glad that initiative key results detect wins and new knowledge earlier in the goal term that can be leveraged right away. There is no reason to wait to the end of the quarter to incorporate new knowledge that may increase current performance.

INITIATIVE OKRS: KEY RESULTS ESSENTIAL (OBJECTIVES OPTIONAL)

What's most important about an initiative OKR is defining the key results. Creating an objective for an initiative can provide clarity, but if teams are experiencing OKR overload, what's most important to focus on is determining the key results for that initiative. Developing explicit objectives can safely be skipped.

Otherwise, creating initiative OKRs is exactly the same as creating organizational ones except typically an initiative has only a single objective (if you're creating one) and one set of key results. The objective, if created, can be in the simple, familiar form of what's most important (the initiative) and why the initiative matters. The key results are the identification of objective measures of progress and success for that initiative to achieve.

For an initiative to be called a success, yes, it must be completed, and it may have one or more milestones that are best set as mandatory goals. But mere completion is not necessarily "success." And, completion of activities also does not necessarily mean "success." I challenge teams to think beyond the activities that they control:

- If you're wildly successful with this initiative, what will be different in the world?
- While you're implementing this initiative, how will you know if you're making progress or going off track?

Since you're thinking about an activity workload, you might be drawn to falling back on what you can control instead of what you can influence to achieve an aspirational, inspirational, changed outcome. Resist that temptation. Ask and answer the same key-result-forming questions as you do for theme-based or functional OKRs. *The answers to the questions may inform an important empirically measurable progress indicator and avoid the problematic watermelon scenario previously discussed.*

You also may want to write activity milestones when you're thinking about your initiatives. Milestones may be important for the working team to have visible; when the most important goal is that something be done by a certain date or a certain number of times, including a milestone in a key result may provide important clarity and alignment. However, if you do so, the best practice is to clearly label it as a milestone, not a key result. The question should always be asked and answered: Is it important that the activity happen a certain number of times or by a date, or is there some other outcome or success criteria the activity should achieve? The key result type can be decided accordingly.

Remember: if you're quantifying activity and identifying milestones, you're planning, not creating empirically measurable key results. In the absence of true key results, you may lack important alignment clarity about what it might mean for the initiative to succeed. Identifying at least one progress key result and at least one outcome key result for each initiative can be essential to giving teams clearer direction.

TRACKING INITIATIVE PROGRESS

Many organizations separate the tracking of organizational/theme-based OKRs and initiative OKRs/project plans. However, if there's a mathematical link between an organizational OKR and an initiative key result (for example, if an initiative is contributing to the performance on an upline key result metric), then a mathematical linkage in the OKR-tracking system is called for. Then, when the team updates their progress in the initiative tracker, the upline key result status is also automatically updated.

That said, it's fairly rare for that condition to be the case. Often initiative key results are metrics that may contribute to your company key result progress but are not the same metric, mathematically connected. Teams may opt to create a template for communicating consistent status information about those initiative key results. It's not necessary to try to force-fit math for the sake of a dashboard linked via the central OKR tracking system if a link to a status update is more useful.

Some OKR specialty software includes the ability to track initiatives as nested children of OKRs. If you're in an environment that doesn't have a work planning system—Trello, ADO, Monday, Smartsheet, or any number of the other project management systems that are typically used in organizations to organize shared work—you may need the additional software. Adding shared work planning to your operational stack can be a huge leap forward in clarity for the organization in terms of expectations around dates, delivery, and details of your work and its progress.

Avoid allowing tracking to become an end in itself.

However, including project management details in your OKR system can create a dynamic in that system where people associate the system with activity and lose focus on the all-important outcomes in their OKRs. Avoid allowing tracking to become an end in itself.

Case in point: Visibility for aligned activities as L3+

Due to confidentiality obligations I'm not allowed to name most clients and must anonymize examples. I'm grateful that early in 2024, I had the privilege to share the stage at the global OKR Forum with Cindy (White) Shea, VP of Operational Excellence at the global education company Pearson and leader of the Pearson OKR Center of Excellence (for the case study we presented, visit findrc.co/okrforump24). (Cindy also wrote the foreword for this book.) I'm glad both to be able to share this example with you and to give Cindy, her team, and her leadership a shout-out as among the most talented and dedicated OKR centers of excellence I've worked with.

Cindy and I have now collaborated on OKR implementation for going on four years. Early in our work together, and after a few quarters of iterating an OKR implementation localized from Level 1 to Level 3 using traditional methods of localization, we noticed the pattern discussed earlier of having very few Level 3 key results and a large number of initiatives at Level 3 that aligned to upline OKRs for which executives needed routine visibility into progress and risks.

Cindy and her team developed a simple, linked spreadsheet template approach that evolved into what they now call the Activity Tracker. A Level 3 or Initiative Activity Tracker identifies and provides a way to collect progress information about aligned initiative key results as well as status information about the progress of the activity of the initiative. From their central OKR tracker (in Smartsheet at the time of print), an executive can click a link to the Activity Tracker for initiatives aligned to the central system of OKRs.

It may require some dual entry if your workload is managed in some other project management or ticket system, but compared to the labor of including Level 3+ "OKRs"[45] in an OKR platform, the labor at the team level to update a spreadsheet once a week or once a month with any relevant key result progress and a brief progress report on the work progress on the aligned initiative(s) is relatively trivial for the value it provides.

Then, the activity tracker can become the linkage for visibility into your initiative progress and risks for all initiatives aligned to your OKRs, without making the OKR system itself overly complicated (or watered down into a glorified project management system instead of being focused truly on OKRs).

With this approach, the central OKR tracker can have a link out to activity trackers for any initiatives that align to the OKRs.

The Activity Tracker then lets cross-functional partners and upline leaders see at a glance at any time the latest update on that initiative's progress.

It's been a simple solution to a typically challenging problem. As Pearson's OKR implementation grows and expands, they are reaching the critical mass of transitioning to an OKR specialty platform—but working with their homegrown tracking systems as they normalize OKRs to their environment will make it so much easier for them to identify their use cases and ultimately choose an OKR platform with confidence that it will solve the challenges they're having with their homegrown system that truly works for their implementation.

---

[45]   In quotes because, as discussed previously, most of what is actually tracked at Level 3+ are not actually objectives or key results and are more likely milestones and initiatives.

TL^DR: STRATEGIST TAKEAWAYS

- Initiatives identify the major workloads that are how you'll achieve your OKR progress and outcomes.
- Initiatives may have objectives (optionally) and key results (recommended) to make clear and quantifiable the measures of progress and success that are most important for each initiative to contribute to your OKRs.

13

ALIGNED INDIVIDUAL GOALS

According to Gallup,[46] in the United States, worker engagement (the involvement and enthusiasm of employees in their work and workplace) is on the decline. From 2019 to 2022, engagement elements that employees reported as declining the most included:

- Connection to the mission or purpose of the company.
- Opportunities to learn and grow.
- Clarity of expectations.
- Opportunities to do what employees do best.

Decades of research has shown that traditional approaches to evaluation and incentivization in the workplace run counter to important performance factors such as intrinsic motivation and ethical, high-integrity workplace behavior, but not a lot has actually changed. The

---

[46]   Jim Harter, "U.S. Employee Engagement Needs a Rebound in 2023," Gallup.com, January 25, 2023, findrc.co/gal2023EErep.

2020 pandemic finally disrupted that status quo, and now employers focused on performance are updating their approaches to management, incentives, and rewards.

WHY NOT TO ADOPT OKRS

It's painfully common, I'm afraid, for OKRs to be introduced in an organization because senior leadership wants to increase the output of the do-ers in the organization without having to evaluate themselves and the role they play in organizational productivity. As a result, two of the most common questions I'm asked are:

- "How—practically—do we localize OKRs down to each individual in the company?"
- "How can we link performance evaluation and individual incentives to OKRs?"

And the simple answer I provide in response to both questions loses me a fair amount of business (which is fine by me):

- "You don't."

WHAT ABOUT INDIVIDUAL ACCOUNTABILITY AND INDIVIDUAL OKRS?

Traditional OKR models may attempt to cascade all the way down to the individual. But have you ever seen any system cascading down that far that wasn't full of assigned activities instead of clear, empirically measurable outcomes and expectations? (If, in fact, you've been looking.) Probably not. Me neither.

Cascading OKRs down to the individual and continuing to call them objectives and key results guarantees the erosion of key result integrity. It's reasonable to create speculative stretch goals for the collective—the whole is greater than the sum of its parts—but at the individual level, goals need to be absolutely clear about what is expected.

> **Cascading OKRs down to the individual and continuing to call them objectives and key results guarantees the erosion of key result integrity.**

It's not possible (outside of sales and a few other scenarios) to consistently and fairly set a threshold for the measurable outcome an individual must achieve to be considered successful in their role, so inevitably at the individual goal level, the integrity of key results gives way to subjectively evaluated goals that are not key results. The desire to cascade goals all the way to the individual rarely exists for the purpose of increasing the empowerment of that individual. Instead, it's often to control and micromanage, or worse, it's a futile attempt to impose a more "objective" method for individual evaluation because some people are not performing to expectations.

Most OKR experts agree that there should be some space between organizational OKR attainment and individual evaluation. To begin to understand why, let's take a thoughtful look at individual goals.

WHY USE ALIGNED INDIVIDUAL GOALS?

Individual goals are important for clarity of expectations, motivation, evaluation, and rewards—and ultimately for achievement of the organization's goals. Individuals need to know what's expected of them, with clarity. Ideally, self-set individual goals are in line with a person's intrinsic motivation and career/growth goals. These goals are the last link in the chain that answers the ever-important question: "Does my work matter?"

Without your people hitting their marks, your organization is unlikely to achieve its organizational goals. Most organizations, therefore, need some way to manage performance. Individual goals may—if thoughtfully structured and evaluated—provide a basis for performance evaluation and development. Individual goals and their attainment also often play a role in incentive pay and rewards calculations.

I will address the topic of performance management here, with a caveat. It breaks my brain that organizations rely so heavily on individual goals that are self-set to inform incentives and rewards. There's an inherent risk of unfair arbitrariness when basing rewards on self-set goals. I would rather see leaders give their reports direction on goal setting while communicating clear performance expectations. Then people can create self-set growth and development goals for the purpose of learning, not primarily for evaluation.

In an ideal world, all organizations would have excellent leadership that is skilled in the nuances of individual performance and growth, and each leader could be trusted to evaluate their reports in the way that makes sense for their discipline. The outcome would be a fair, high-performing system with happy employees. High performers are rewarded and retained; low performers are coached and developed (or managed into roles where

> **In an ideal world, all organizations would have excellent leadership skilled in the nuances of individual performance and growth.**

they can be more successful). The middle is either happily humming along in their run-the-business modes to collect their paycheck twice a month or is coached to increase the likelihood they'll step up into the high-performance zone.

In my dreams. Not all organizations are able to stitch together the procedures, learning and development infrastructure, and modeled leader behavior to achieve this vision. So let's talk about scenarios that are a little more down to earth.

I'll be the first to disclaim: I am not a human resources consultant, nor am I a researcher in the field of performance management. I'm an OKR coach and leadership development pro who is asked by almost every client I work with to reconcile their group and individual goal setting practices. My approach comes at these questions through an "operationalizing for goal achievement" lens.

The best practices shared here have been implemented by my clients with ongoing success. They serve as a starting place for your own organization's re-examination of your performance management practices.

BEST PRACTICES FOR INDIVIDUAL GOALS IN THE NO-BS OKR ENVIRONMENT

The most important best practices I coach in the area of individual goals and performance management are:

- Be mindful of the behaviors that individual and group goal setting, performance evaluation, and rewards practices are designed to drive.
- Create some separation between the attainment of group OKRs and individual performance evaluation to ensure

courageous, stretch group OKR creation and a consistent, predictable, and fair individual performance evaluation model.

- Let go of trying to localize OKRs down to the individual; doing so may be arbitrary and nonsensical at scale.

- Take effort toward OKRs and individual stretch goals into account, along with performance on RTB/milestones-based mandatory goals. The evaluation rubric should ensure fairness across different role types (and shouldn't disincentivize ambitious goal setting).

- Ensure transparency about how incentives are funded and calculated.

Incentivized behaviors

Too frequently, performance management practices are variable across leadership and uncomfortably subjective. Leaders may even unfairly reward employees they like or who are more "like them." Subjective assessment encourages some of the most damaging "managing up" behaviors,[47] including overemphasizing being "pleasing" to the supervising leader, sometimes at the expense of the work itself and often not in the organization's best interest compared to encouraging a focus on delivery of excellent work.

These risks create the craving for numbers-based evaluation models (and hence, linking OKRs and performance management), which you might think you're getting by cascading OKRs to the individual. But when individual evaluation and incentives are linked to

---

[47]   To learn more about my take on the common coaching around "managing up" as an essential workplace skill and replacing that coaching with an emphasis on learning self-management skills, check out the two-part podcast series on the downsides of managing up, in Episodes 02 and 03 of the Thinkydoers podcast: findrc.co/4eILu9W and findrc.co/481Z4Tz .

self-set numerical goals, two things might occur: those who sandbag their own goals may be rewarded as high performers because they've purposely set their goals to easy-to-reach levels (making their numbers "look good"); and those who set ambitious goals and work hard to achieve them may be penalized with lower rewards even if their overall contribution is higher than their sandbagging colleagues.

> **Carefully examine the implications of your individual evaluation and incentives model and watch carefully for disincentives and areas of unacceptable bias.**

There is no easy answer here. The bottom line is to carefully examine the implications of your individual evaluation and incentives model and watch carefully for disincentives and areas of unacceptable bias. Perhaps invest in leadership development to enhance upper management's people skills for evaluating and managing reports to bring your organization closer to the ideal envisioned at the top of this section.

Separate group OKRs and individual performance evaluation

Building on the last section, I agree with other leading sources in recommending distance between the attainment of organizational OKRs and determination of individual performance management.[48]

---

[48] See e.g., www.whatmatters.com/articles/laszlo-bock-divorce-compensation-from-okrs.

> **You want your OKRs to encourage ambitiously stretching together to take your organization to a whole new level of growth, improvement, and performance.**

Having individual rewards tied closely to the numerical attainment of your group or shared key results encourages conservative goal setting. In that case, people are incentivized to set goals they know they can achieve; this is the antithesis of legitimate OKRs, which need to be stretch. You want your OKRs to encourage ambitiously stretching together to take your organization to a whole new level of growth, improvement, and performance. For that to be the case, you and your people must be safe to try—and even fail—at your objectives and key results, in the pursuit of experimentation and learning.

When group OKRs have distance from individual performance management, your organization can rally together to generate mutual support and cheer each other on. When things are challenging or when you're having one of those particularly interesting learning experiences, you'll know you're in it together. That's not going to be the case if the people involved are worrying about their personal bonus or likelihood of promotion.

In the group goal setting—when you're using OKRs in the No-BS model—you set ambitious goals to the tips of your fingers of what's possible. You ask: "What would be amazing to achieve if everything goes right?" Then you harness the curiosity, inspiration, and motivation those goals encourage and get to work, doing your best to make as much progress as possible. If you don't achieve the goal, then you ask yourself what you can learn. You reset your goal, and try again.

But in the individual goal arena, organizations rely on performance to evaluate an individual. There are consequences of underperforming, both for organizational impact and each person's career growth and incentive pay.

OKRs and individual goals are like two different animals: meerkats and tigers.[49]

Group OKRs	Individual Goals

"We want to set ambitious, inspired goals, because that's how we achieve the most together."

"I want to set goals I know I can achieve to earn my bonus."

Mostly stretch	⟷	Mostly stretch
We're safe to try, and fail—if we miss the mark, we learn	⟷	We're typically not "safe" to fail—there may be serious consequences
Mindset = curiosity + learning	⟷	Mindset = judgment + evaluation

Meerkats live in large groups and rely on each other for survival, with each member of the group having a specific role: foraging for food, keeping watch for predators, or caring for young. Tigers are solitary hunters and usually live and roam alone (except during mating season, or when a mother is raising her cubs).

When working on your group OKRs, use your meerkat brain. You can afford group goals to be stretch because the whole is greater than

49   I first used this analogy in my courses with Section School, including my Strategic Planning Sprint with them that I'm very proud of. For more information, visit: findrc.co/section_sara.

the sum of its parts. You're safe to try and even fail, to operate with a curious learning mindset because of the relative safety of the collective. Your meerkat brains say: "We want to set ambitious, inspired goals because that's how we'll all be the most successful together."

On the other hand, when working on individual goals, most people tend to be focused first on what must be achieved to maximize their individual potential and bonus or incentives, with the collective good as a second priority. Most people are more comfortable identifying milestones and mandatory goals, sometimes set as empirically measurable goals, but always at a threshold they believe they can safely achieve. Individuals may not be "safe to fail" on milestones or mandatory goals; there may be serious consequences for non-achievement. So in individual goals, people are much more in their tiger brains. They are aware of their singular responsibility for their own "care and feeding"—more of a survival brain state: heightened vigilance, judgment, and evaluation. They're not as consciously wired for learning because learning may come with risks. The tiger brain says: "I want to set goals I know I can achieve in order to maximize my bonus."

Group OKRs and individual goals—even aligned individual goals—are rooted in different questions.

- In group OKRs, you're asking: "What are our most important objectives? How will we know if we're making progress or success? How can we set ambitious, inspired goals, to maximize our achievement together?"
- In individual goals, you're asking: "How does my work support our OKRs? How might I learn and develop or grow in a way that boosts my career and the organization? What goals can I set to show my contribution but I know I can achieve in order to earn my bonus?"

Group OKRs and individual goals are two different animals. Individual goals may align up to the organization OKRs. Ideally, individuals would look up the food chain to consider how they can maximally support the

Group OKRs and individual goals are two different animals.

organization's OKRs (and other strategic inputs). But the two types of goals require different operations and evaluation standards. It makes sense to think of group OKRs and individual goals as two different (though perhaps linked) things, treated differently by the practices and procedures of your organization.

Let go of the idea of localization to the individual

While sometimes it may make sense for salespeople or executive leaders to have commission- or performance-based pay packages, for other positions it can be problematic to link individual performance to OKR attainment elsewhere in the organization.

A key factor is responsibility. If an organization localizes OKRs down to every individual, it would be necessary to apportion responsibility mathematically through roll-downs to every person in the organization. This approach is: operationally difficult (if possible at all); arbitrary (Is Sally in Customer Support responsible for 0.05% of the organization's customer retention or 0.07%? Is James in Marketing responsible for 1% or 2%?); and the math breaks every time someone joins or leaves the organization.

Still, while it may make sense to roll down key results to roles where the math adds up, even in the simplest of these scenarios—sales—it's not that simple. Theoretically, your revenue target at Level 1 can be localized to regions at Level 2 and then perhaps down to individual salespeople at Level 3. But even here you have to check yourself. Is the Level 1 revenue number a stretch goal? If so, on what threshold for success will you evaluate your salespeople? Is their target a mandatory or a stretch target? Are they safe to try, and even fail? (Most likely not: If your sellers are safe to try and even fail, your revenue forecast may be too unreliable to operate sustainably.)

Instead, again, try to think of group OKRs and individual goals as two very distinct (if linked) things, with quite different purposes and practices.

Individuals may not always measure success in true key results

Individuals may have a larger number of important "maintain" goals, activity or milestone mandatory goals, and run-the-business goals or responsibilities that should factor into their individual performance evaluation (but don't belong in OKRs).

If individuals were to focus entirely on stretch, hypothetical, localized-to-the-individual-level key results, the machinery of your organization may come to a screeching halt. Where organizational OKRs are predominantly stretch, individual goals necessarily contain more mandatory goals. Individuals often deliver the work that make up dependencies to their colleagues' performance. To leave what an employee must do out of their performance equation makes no sense.

Also recognize that stretch goals by definition take you into unknown and uncertain territory. People may lack the autonomy, authority, capacity, and resources to achieve their experimental, speculative stretch goals. While individual stretch goal setting is critically important for individual growth, career fulfillment, and development for many employees, you can only hope to fairly evaluate a person's effort toward their stretch goal, not their attainment of the number itself.[50]

But what if a person *wants* to write their own objectives and key results for their work? Can they? Of course!

INDIVIDUAL ALIGNED GOALS DISTINGUISHED FROM PERSONAL OKRS

When setting your own aligned individual goals in the workplace, set them according to the guidelines provided by your organization and leadership. If you want to write some in the form of either objectives or key results and that fits the organizational norms, by all means do so. You gain all of the benefits of working with OKRs we've discussed up to this point whether you're working with OKRs in a group or by yourself.

Frequently, when I work with clients over the long term, at a certain point they'll confide excitedly that they created some secret OKRs just for themselves about their work or career and that those personal, secret goals have become a source of motivation and increased engagement.

I also love the nearly inevitable moment when there is a pause in the conversation, and the client asks (usually somewhat sheepishly), "I've been thinking about creating OKRs to improve my parenting/

---

[50]   I've done quite a lot of work with organizations on the technical details of aligning their group goal approaches and individual goal and performance management approaches to encourage desired behaviors and increase fairness of individual recognition and rewards. This is beyond the scope of this book, but if you're a leader or human resources professional responsible for the intersection of group and individual goals and you'd like to see some examples of what I've seen work for clients, visit findrc.co/perf_mgmt for an FAQ on this subject.

motivate a new workout routine/get ready for an upcoming expedition/work with my spouse on our marriage. Is that weird? Can I do that?"

And my answer is always: "*Of course* you can do that."

I consider these "personal OKRs." They sit separate from the organization's system of OKRs and even separate from aligned individual goals you may have set to align your workplace goals to the organizational OKRs. They may relate to your personal life, or they may be work-related.

Personal OKRs are objectives and key results you create personally and usually privately—only for you and purely for your own reasons. Personal OKRs can be motivating, encouraging, and have all the benefits we've talked about with other types of well-formed, inspired, challenging goals.

Personal OKRs can also be a beneficial way to practice creating and working with OKRs. Without oversight from a leader or the prying eyes of cross-functional partners, you can feel more free to experiment without any concern what anyone else thinks. If there is a type of goal you're nervous about, you can try it out personally and see what you learn.

For example, I worked with empirically measurable outcome and progress key results personally for some time before I introduced those concepts to anyone else. It took me some practice to figure out how to write measurable goals. In doing so, I realized that for me, it was more motivating to set measurable goals and try to achieve them (whether I succeeded or failed) than to just work toward an arbitrary work plan or with no success criteria at all. I tended to see more and more

> **Personal OKRs can also be a beneficial way to practice creating and working with OKRs**

enthusiastic progress on my key results than on the milestones and activity-based goals I created for myself, which often became stale before the end of the goal cycle.

By the time I introduced the concept of objectives and key results to my colleagues and teammates, I knew that I'd rather accept the risks of failing on empirically measurable goals than the frustrations of working toward traditional arbitrary success criteria. I could lead and model courage, perseverance, curiosity, and intellectual humility in my pursuit of goals, setting a "walk the talk" example for my colleagues.

If you are working with objectives and key results with other people, words and meanings matter a great deal to achieve shared understanding. If you are creating personal OKRs on your own, the rules can go out the window. Use whatever pieces of OKR practice you think may be work; experiment wildly and see what you learn; take what works for you and leave what you don't. In a single-user environment, personal OKRs do not have to follow any rules. Do whatever keeps you motivated and engaged—just be sure to keep track of your new knowledge so you can improve over time.

TL^DR: STRATEGIST TAKEAWAYS

- Aligned individual goals are essential for individual clarity of expectations, individual motivation, and for achievement of the organization's goals. Without them, your organization is highly unlikely to achieve its organizational goals.

- Best practices for aligned individual goals in a Rebelutionary organization include:

  - Being mindful of the behaviors individual and group goal setting, performance evaluation, and rewards practices are designed to drive.

- Ensuring separation between group OKRs and the individual's performance evaluation to ensure stretch group OKR creation and a consistent, predictable, generally fair individual performance evaluation model.
- OKRs localized down to the individual are not aligned individual goals; this may lead to arbitrary and nonsensical attempts to apportion down to the individual.
- Watch out for:
  - Disincentives from linking individual evaluation or rewards to the attainment of OKRs.
  - Evaluation schemes that risk under-rewarding desired behavior and over-rewarding undesired behavior.
- Personal OKRs are OKRs created purely for your own focus, clarity, and inspiration. They don't have to align to your organization's OKRs, and they may be a fantastic way to practice OKRs (and gain the benefits of OKRs for your personal career and way beyond).

14

STRATEGY IS CHANGING BEHAVIOR

Want to know one of the things humans are even worse at than estimating their progress?

Changing their behavior.

Before I began my course of study in health and wellness coaching in 2021, I devoured the book *Immunity to Change* by Robert Kegan and Lisa Laskow Lahey. They mention research completed at Johns Hopkins University that found "when doctors tell heart patients they will die if they don't change their habits, only one in seven will be able to follow through successfully."

The status quo is strong. Even in matters of life and death, humans are creatures of habit.

When I ask people in business what gets in the way of achieving their goals, I hear a variety of answers:

- "Market factors beyond our control."
- "Lack of resources, capacity, or budget to do what we need."

- "Micromanaging leaders getting stuck in the weeds, becoming a bottleneck."
- "Conflicting corporate processes that aren't in alignment—our roadmap takes us away from our OKRs focus."
- "There's just so much resistance to the idea of goal setting. People feel more comfortable with checklists of activity."
- "Leaders like to keep their functional details like a black box; if they share measurable goals transparently, they may be held accountable to them, and they don't want to be unless they succeed."

Every organization and every person is going to have a different flavor of local challenge, but the core of what I hear in each of these barriers is a lack of appetite for and readiness to change.

Organizations can be thought of as systems (and they are). But when it comes down to it, an organization's most important strategic element is individual people taking courageous action to experiment, take risks, and ultimately demonstrate new behavior.

Solid strategic planning practices support those behaviors; behavior change supports strategy achievement.

While independently developed, the practices you've learned through this book so far align to a foundation of findings from motivation and behavioral science. They are also strongly influenced by my more recent 2021 training as a health and wellness coach—a relatively new professional specialty that helps people like the ones mentioned in *Immunity to Change* plot their way through recovery or lifestyle change.

"Health and wellness coaches engage individuals and groups in evidence-based, client-centered processes that facilitate and empower clients to develop and achieve self-determined, health and wellness goals."[51]

I chose my professional coach training program in 2021 based on many of the instructors being authors I follow in positive psychology circles. It was there, after I'd developed nearly all the practices you've learned in this book, that I learned how closely these practices align to what is known about motivation in behavioral science.

FOUR FACTORS THAT AFFECT GOAL ATTAINMENT

Achieving your strategy requires changing behavior. If you're a visionary leader, achieving your strategy means enabling other people to change their behavior. Neither of these are easy tasks. So if there's a little science that can make you more effective, why not look into it? Let's look at four factors that affect goal attainment through the behavioral science lens.

1. Bolster goal persistence by choosing performance-enhancing goal thresholds.
2. Normalize curiosity about objective progress data.
3. Don't try to go it alone.
4. Nurture intrinsic motivation; don't over rely on extrinsic motivation and feedback.

---

[51] Source: NBHWC Scope of Practice: nbhwc.org/scope-of-practice/. The National Board for Health and Wellness Coaching (NBHWC) is the certifying and governing body for health and wellness coaches in the United States.

1. Bolster goal persistence by choosing performance-enhancing goal thresholds

Different people have different levels of goal persistence or its flip side: the rate at which people get frustrated into ending their goal pursuit. You may have seen this play out on teams you've worked with, where one person throws up their hands at the mere mention of the first challenge the team faces: "Well, that's impossible. It can't be done." A few weeks later, when the project is well underway and an obstacle that indicates that our skeptic may have been right—it may *actually be impossible*—another voice in the room insists: "But we're so close, we just have to look at this problem in a different way. Let's give the team a little more time."

People's personal degree of goal persistence is variable, but science says that you can bolster goal persistence by setting goals at challenging but not impossible thresholds.

Contrary to the argument I hear all the time from leaders that setting goals at a stretch level that you aren't positive you can achieve is discouraging, what the science says is that when goals are too easy they don't provide enough stimulation to keep people engaged. However, if goals are perceived as "impossible," people may become frustrated and disengage. "Nothing hinders the change process more than setting unrealistic and unachievable goals."[52]

> **"Nothing hinders the change process more than setting unrealistic and unachievable goals."**

So this is the job of collaborative goal setting: to identify the threshold for a goal at which it's challenging

52   Moore, M., Jackson, E., and Tschannen-Moran, B., *Coaching Psychology Manual* (2nd ed., p. 133), Wolters Kluwer, 2016.

enough to encourage goal persistence but not so challenging as to be believed to be impossible.

When presenting a stretch goal, you can anticipate someone responding like our skeptic above: "That's impossible!" Be ready with your rationale as to why you believe that threshold is a healthy stretch, how pursuit of that goal will be supported with resources, and what your basis was for selecting it. You won't convince every skeptic with persuasion; skeptics may need more time to get used to the idea and to observe quick wins to change their position. Analogizing to coaching practice, tell your team that their potential is often greater than they realize. Aside from your most persistent skeptics, people may be inspired by being called to a vision that's greater than what they thought possible.

> **When presenting a stretch goal, you can anticipate someone responding "That's impossible!" Be ready with your rationale.**

Goal threshold is also important because people "experience flow when their goals are challenging slightly beyond their skills and experience"[53] and flow is a generative, creative, productive state that many wish to feel more of in their work.

2. Normalize curiosity about objective progress data

In some workplaces, leaders only want to hear the good news and challenging them is a risky proposition. "Come to me with solutions, not problems" is a familiar refrain. It wasn't until I was an executive leader myself that I really grasped the magnitude of how wrong this is. For intellectually humble Rebelutionary leaders, it's important to

---

[53] Ibid., *Coaching Psychology*, p. 135.

foster a culture of openness and transparency where issues can be raised early, before they become major risks or setbacks.

In the absence of data that reveals how you're performing, strategic achievement is a crapshoot. We've already discussed the risks of relying on an "estimate of completion." In its place, get curious and creative about what indicators let you know where you are and in which direction you're going.

Calmly and curiously assessing meaningful progress data for important major outcomes—even when the numbers "look bad"—may be the single biggest contributor to improved strategic achievement possible.

> "[The] ability to monitor oneself is a key factor in goal achievement. . . . [I]t is important not only to elicit qualitative feedback regarding client progress but also to track outcomes delivered by establishing new behaviors in objective, measurable terms."[54]

Identifying leading indicators is one of the most challenging parts of creating OKRs, but it's also the worthiest to invest time in. Progress on one goal increases the chance that other goals may be achieved. When setbacks are considered normal and a way to learn, that's when a culture kicks truly into high performance.

3. Don't try to go it alone

I am (sometimes affectionately, sometimes not) referred to by friends and family, as a "lone wolf." I have a sometimes pathological independent streak and am for the most part resigned to self-sufficiency.

---

[54]   Ibid., *Coaching Psychology* (citing MacKenzie, Mezo, and Francis, 2012), p. 137.

In earlier phases of my life, if I couldn't do it alone, then it wasn't meant for me to do. When I learned the below standard sequence of coaching questions, I quickly learned and practiced it—with one notable exception.

The sequence of questions was[55]:

1. What is your goal?
2. What steps or options will you take before our next session?
3. What obstacles may arise?
4. Who can you recruit for support or assistance in navigating those obstacles?
5. What specific behaviors do you commit to make, and by when?

Yep, Number 4 was my downfall. I had to keep a sticky note in view—stuck to my monitor frame—with "Who can you ask for help?" on it. (And that sticky note stayed attached to my monitor long after I completed my training.)

Research consistently shows that social support can significantly enhance behavior change and goal achievement. Two major theories of change center social support. The social cognitive theory of change (SCT) centers environmental factors (including support networks and role models) between the two more expected factors that determine human behavior: personal (beliefs) and behavioral (experiences and accomplishments).[56] The self-determination theory of change includes relatedness—relationships—as one of three primary psychological needs

[55]   This set of questions derives from the Auerbach GOOD Coaching Model, created by Jeffrey E. Auerbach, Ph.D., MCC, President of the College of Executive Coaching.

[56]   For more information, check out Bandura, A., and National Institute of Mental Health, *Social Foundations of Thought and Action: A Social Cognitive Theory*, Prentice-Hall, Inc., 1986.

for autonomous self-regulation of behavior. Self-determination theory has been described as "the most respected theory of human motivation today, which also addresses primary human needs and well-being."[57]

> **When you share goals or share your goal with someone else, it creates a sense of shared responsibility, support, and motivation.**

When working with others, each can serve as the others' accountability partner. When you share goals or share your goal with someone else and routinely keep each other updated on your progress, it creates a sense of shared responsibility, support, and motivation. You're in it together and won't let each other fail. It's easier to see setbacks as gathering new information when a kind collaborator reminds you to do so.

During my advertising career, in moments of crisis or high stakes opportunity, a "rapid response room" was convened, to harness the magic that happens when people come together in shared problem-solving. It was in those rooms that I saw firsthand a group of people pull off something that would have definitely been impossible for any one individual to do alone.

Goal setting and sustained goal pursuit or efforts to change behavior may be pursued as a solo activity. But when obstacles arise, turn to the trusted others around you. Even if you are, like me, a "lone wolf," this is a reminder not to try to go it alone on goals and behavior change.

---

[57]   *Coaching Psychology*, p. 11, referring to the Self-Determination Theory developed by Edward Deci and Richard Ryan.

4. Nurture intrinsic motivation; don't over-rely on extrinsic motivation and feedback.

Those of us who read motivation science research scratch our head at many workplace norms: especially around intrinsic and extrinsic motivation. Research by Edward Deci and co-authors Richard Koestner and Richard M. Ryan's "A meta-analytic review of experiments examining the effects of extrinsic rewards on intrinsic motivation"[58] is such a worthwhile read, I'm not relegating its findings to a footnote here.

In a meta-analysis of 128 studies, Deci and colleagues found that extrinsic rewards such as money or prizes generally *undermine* intrinsic motivation in situations involving complex and interesting tasks like the ones involved in much of our work today[59] and may have a positive effect on intrinsic motivation only for uninteresting activities.[60] All types of tangible rewards—including money—were found to decrease intrinsic motivation. In contrast, positive feedback was found to enhance intrinsic motivation. Extrinsic rewards may boost short-term performance on repetitive tasks, but only certain jobs are compensated that way. In any setting when an extrinsic reward is used and then removed, people experience a decrease in intrinsic interest in whatever they were previously incentivized to do.

Now, the lion's share of academic research was conducted on college students, not in modern workplaces. But from what I see in workplaces every day, the same holds true for people at work.

[58] Deci, E.L., Koestner, R., Ryan, R.M., "A Meta-analytic Review of Experiments Examining the Effects of Extrinsic Rewards on Intrinsic Motivation," *Psychological Bulletin,* November 1999.

[59] Ibid., p. 630.

[60] Ibid., p. 632.

Autonomy is a critical factor in self-determination, alongside competence and relatedness.[61] Providing people autonomy, room to connect with their intrinsic motivation, and freedom to self-set inspired, aspirational goals that align to the organization's goals is foundational to building an organizational culture where people are invested in the work they do (beyond just a paycheck).

A virtuous system of self-determination, self-efficacy, and social support create the conditions for individual behavior change. Individual behavior change is what separates you from your current status quo and your aspirational strategic achievement.

BREAKING THE INERTIA OF COMFORT

Keep the four factors mentioned above in mind when you're architecting the policies and procedures that make up your organizational culture. The inertia habit, the comfort of the status quo, may present formidable barriers to organizational change. It's through the deliberate, courageous, mindful actions of each person that your strategic achievement is advanced.

Strategic achievement is not about beautiful slides being presented in boardrooms; it's about the subtle shifts in behavior that ripple through an organization, inspiring innovation, increasing performance impact, and catching people's eyes: "Well, if she can do that, maybe I can."

It's the leader's job to foster an environment where behavior change is recognized as a learning process and not taken for granted, but encouraged. Each step forward, even when learning from setbacks, is a step toward increased strategic achievement.

---

[61]   This is a foundation of Deci and Ryan's self-determination theory, which, if you want to go deep on, check out: Ryan, R. M., and Deci, E. L., *Self-Determination Theory: Basic Psychological Needs in Motivation, Development, and Wellness*, Guilford Press, 2017. doi. org/10.1521/978.14625/28806

TL^DR: STRATEGIST TAKEAWAYS

- Strategy achievement doesn't happen without individual behavior change; but workplace practices and conditions often hinder change.

- Individual acts of courage and behavior change are what move you forward.

- Goal setting, intrinsic motivation, and learning from setbacks are critical for progress and strategic achievement.

- To create conditions for successful behavior change, focus on four factors:

  1. Creating conditions for goal persistence by choosing challenging but not impossible goal thresholds.
  2. Get comfortable with and curious about objective progress data.
  3. Don't try to go it alone.
  4. Nurture conditions for intrinsic motivation and autonomy.

15

IMPLEMENTING OKRS

Want to know what bakes my noodle?

Even though many OKR implementations get to the end of Chapter 9: "Creating No-BS Key Results" and just stop there . . .

Even though leaders and teams put extensive effort into creating their OKRs, sharing them on a slide at a town hall, setting up Excel spreadsheets or OKR platforms to track their progress, but then everybody wakes up the next day, sits down at their desks, and goes to work on business as usual, as if nothing ever happened . . .

Even though at the end of the quarter, if they're lucky, an over-achiever OKR core team member might schedule a quarterly review, creating a flurry of activity where presenters have to report on their OKR progress, even though they haven't looked at their OKRs since they were written . . .

. . . even then, each of what I just described above can improve organizational performance.

There is not a lot of research on OKRs, since there is no standardized implementation practice. But one study from a call center at Sears from 2013 gets cited frequently. That study found that even with set-and-forget OKRs, performance improved by 3%, compared to teams that didn't create OKRs.[62]

In OKR circles, I've heard of data showing a 19% increase in performance when OKRs are implemented with a routine rhythm for actively managing their progress (but haven't been able to find a citation for that, so take it with a grain of salt). The potential for increased goal attainment with implementation of a recurring rhythm of business leading to a near-20% increase in performance is believable for me, based on what I've seen among my clients.

> **There's little sense in spending the time to create OKRs then failing to operationalize a rhythm to achieve your best possible performance.**

There's little sense in spending the time to create OKRs then failing to operationalize a rhythm to achieve your best possible performance.

Let's first look at who the essential players are to implementing a connected strategy successfully; then we'll spend a moment on tracking. But most of this chapter will focus on what's critical and often underestimated: the importance of changing behavior by formalizing a goal-achievement focused rhythm of business.

WHO IT TAKES

Most resources on OKRs will begin by describing the important features of a successful OKR core team, but we're going to begin somewhere else.

---

[62] Ben Lamorte has a great write-up on this study on his excellent website, okrs. com. Source: okrs.com/2015/03/sears-holding-company-study-concludes-okrs-impact-the-bottom-line/.

Early OKR implementations often rely heavily on program management in the form of an OKR core team or champion to execute the OKR rhythm of business. Core team members tend to pull the organization along—sending out reminders, filling gaps in incomplete work from leaders and teams, and carrying a lot of labor of executing the OKR rhythm.

Leaders may delegate parts of OKR creation and administration and often over rely on the core team's labor, treating OKRs as an administrative process instead of a fundamental responsibility of leadership.

This is wrong.

Instead, it's the leaders who must be involved at every step of the process.

A successful OKR implementation requires leaders who walk the talk

A mature OKR adoption requires leaders to lead on OKR rhythms. There may at first be an organizational learning phase facilitated by a coach, consultant, or OKR platform, but ultimately it's the leaders who make it happen.

This may sound idealistic, but OKRs are meant to be useful for leaders. If they aren't, why on earth would you spend this kind of time and effort on another strategic goal pageant? OKRs should yield important information about your progress and risks; therefore, it's the role of leaders to ensure that OKRs are high quality, are complete and aligned, and model best practices for their organization.

In a No-BS OKR organization:

1. Leaders bring vision, direction, focus, and rigor to OKR creation and see OKRs as an essential part of establishing clear expectations for their teams and partners.

2. Leaders supervise their reports' OKR creation and review reports' candidate OKRs for alignment.

3. Leaders run OKR rhythms with little oversight from core team members, and they communicate OKRs to their organizations via town hall meetings and OKR progress via their rhythms.

4. Leaders handle performance and quality issues themselves, rather than delegating.

A skilled OKR core team is essential

OKR coaches and core team members provide methodology expertise, coaching, and workshop facilitation to support OKR creation. The core team leads the OKR rhythm (with reasonable reminders) and the core team maintains systems for OKR tracking and progress communication.

If there is a gap, the core team doesn't fill it; they allow the gap to be visible. That way, leadership can assess who's responsible, set clear expectations, and ensure expectations are met.

No-BS OKR core team members:

- Keep the OKR calendar, and send prompts at key times of year, including:
  - OKR creation kick-off.
  - OKR quarterly review preparation.
  - Availability of OKR-related training or workshops.
- Serve as internal experts on the OKR methodology.

- Are not creators of OKRs for leaders and teams; they're a valuable source of expertise leaders and teams can turn to for support with OKR creation, administration, communication, and learning.

No-BS OKR coaches:

- Guide others as specially trained experts[63] with deep expertise in the OKR methodology and creation.
- Expertly ask questions designed to prompt team members toward creating their own inspired, aspirational OKRs.
- Are not experts in the business; they rarely offer suggestions about potential objectives and key results.
- Bring a "yes, and" style to coaching, tailoring their support to each leader and team they work with, to be encouraging and supportive of their goal creation.

Leaders must do their own labor

Hot take: Leaders are responsible for the labor of creating and implementing their OKRs.

When a new organization reaches out to me, it's often in the form of a tired, stressed, burned-out OKR core team member. That team member may have begun the organization's OKR implementation excited and invested, but now they're completely over it. A meeting or two later, when I meet with their leadership team and hear complaints about how poorly the organization is doing at implementing

---

[63] Twice a year, I train OKR coaches in the best practices I use every day myself. For more information and to join the waitlist or nominate someone for the next training, please visit: findrc.co/okrcoachtrain.

OKRs, I launch the conversation that separates the potential Rebelutionary organizations from their more typical peers.

> **Me:** "Can you please tell me about who does the labor of operating your OKR rhythm?"
>
> **Leader:** "The OKR core team," often followed by some grumbles about how the implementation is—or isn't—going.
>
> **Me:** "Who is responsible for articulating your vision and strategy?"
>
> **Leader:** "Senior leadership."
>
> **Me:** "Who is ultimately responsible for creating the goals your organization aspires to achieve?"
>
> **Leader:** [after some mental gymnastics] "Senior leadership."
>
> **Me:** "So if your senior leadership is responsible for articulating your vision and strategy and creating the goals your organization aspires to achieve, who is responsible for the labor of doing those things?"

It's a bit of a trap, I'll admit. But a leadership team that is not willing to do their own labor in the OKR rhythm is not a Rebelutionary leadership team.

A big part of my work is making OKR rhythms simpler so that leaders can drive and own them. The OKR core team operates in an internal expert capacity, not a doer capacity. Leaders—the people ultimately responsible for creating and aligning OKRs—are responsible for the labor of creating and implementing OKRs, with support from their teams and cross-functional partners.

High-functioning OKR core teams often feel responsible for the success of the OKR rhythm and for then

> **A big part of my work is making OKR rhythms simpler so that leaders can drive and own them.**

over-functioning in terms of labor with regard to OKRs. A leader may lag on OKR creation. The internal OKR coach "helps" by writing a first draft for them, so that when it comes time for the alignment review, that leader's page isn't blank. When there is a blank, the senior-most leader often looks at the OKR core team and asks: "Why doesn't this manager have goals in the sheet?" instead of looking at the manager and asking: "Why don't you have goals in the sheet?"

The same characteristics that draw many people to OKR coaching and core-team work are the same characteristics that lead to over-functioning in terms of filling gaps in labor for their leadership. Leaders, in turn, develop a "learned helplessness" about the OKR rhythm, relying heavily on the OKR coaches and core teams to make up the difference.

To maximize an OKR implementation, this dynamic must be avoided. OKR core team members must let leaders and colleagues fail in the creation and administration of their OKRs; the senior-most leader must hold the lagging leaders responsible, not the coach or core team.

Only then do leaders pick up the mantle, get with the program, and take OKRs seriously instead of treating them as an administrative activity.

Resetting labor expectations during an OKR implementation in progress

When an organization is adopting or rebooting an OKR implementation, I use a written document to communicate the purpose of the changes needed, the background, a detail of what's changing, and then clear expectations for "what this means for participants," *and* "what this means for leaders." Here is an example of the latter from a recent OKR Quarterly Review Refresh project with a large enterprise client.

- Be ready to crisply and consistently use key words and meanings (specifically, "milestone" and "key result") accurately so the organization can learn the best practices you're adopting.

- Steer conversations toward outcomes for items where achieving an outcome is important. If a participant is focused on activity in a territory where an outcome is important, begin a brief conversation about potential outcomes they may aim for regarding their Q4 key results.

- When risks, blockers, or needs are raised, take a moment to consider whether it can be addressed live during the meeting or whether a note needs to be taken to resolve as a follow-up (and who should be involved in that follow-up).

- Acknowledge that the responsibility for OKRs lies with leaders and their direct reports: if your report is missing a key result where you think they should have one, flag that and work with them to ensure they have clear direction to create the key result.

- The OKR core team facilitates smooth operations of your rhythms and the meeting; but gaps in information or missing key results are the responsibility of leaders and their teams to address.

- Key result quality and making sure you have key results where you need them is the responsibility of leaders and their reports. The OKR core team can consult around OKR quality, but OKRs are perhaps the most important means to clarify expectations between leaders and their reports so ultimate responsibility sits with leaders and their reports.

When expectations are communicated this clearly, everyone in the system is empowered to speak up if they aren't met or heeded. OKR Core team members share in this authority.

Identified OKR stewards

In addition to leaders walking the talk and OKR experts who can lend subject matter expertise, the final critical cohort are objective and key result stewards: one identified steward per objective and key result.

Most practitioners, tools, and organizations call that person the *owner*, but ownership is too closely associated with having sole responsibility for the effort. I prefer the term *steward*, since that communicates that the person is on point to manage, direct, and keep things moving along but that they are not singularly responsible for the development and achievement of the objectives and key results.

An OKR steward keeps progress moving and brings attention to blockers and risks. An OKR steward is also responsible for knowing the status of the objective or key result and providing updates to other key stakeholders.

Another reason for the subtlety of this word choice is that unlike the idea of an owner (usually whomever is closest to the objective or key result in terms of subject matter expertise),

> **An OKR steward keeps progress moving and brings attention to blockers and risks.**

the idea of a steward is a reminder that stewardship of an objective or key result is a shared responsibility that can rotate or be passed around a team or working group. A group of people working on a key result together could rotate the stewardship responsibility bi-weekly or monthly, which also gives multiple people on the team a chance to practice their executive communication and leadership skills.

However, most OKR software calls this person the owner. If it's not possible to customize this in your system, you can still redefine the OKR owner as occupying the stewardship role I described above.

OKR TRACKING, COMMUNICATION, AND CLARITY AT SCALE

The strongest No-BS OKR implementations I've seen in organizations (large and small):

- Communicate OKRs using the "on one page" approach.
- Identify and manage delivery plans in another system (a project or program management system) that can be linked to OKR tracking but not muddled together with it.
- Track the quantifiable OKR progress and success at Level 1 and Level 2 of the OKRs (as well as any rolled down or rolled up key results at Level 3+) in a standard business tool, OKR specialty platform, or software add-in.
- Track Level 3+ OKRs, initiative progress, and milestones that are not directly from upline OKRs with a link to OKR-aligned initiatives.
- Include accountability concepts, such as options for both ownership and stewardship of goals.

In short: Math rolls up and down. The Level 3+ local tracking is kept routinely up to date; important information about wins, progress, and blockers are routinely communicated to upline leaders, so that the issues have the visibility to direct results and problem-solving. Individual responsibility is established through delivery or work plans and through creation of aligned individual goals by every person in the organization.

With that, an organization may have two levels of OKRs (sometimes three, maximum) tracked centrally. The rest of the organization then reports up their progress, risks, wins, blockers, and needs through their supervisors, who are responsible for ensuring teams have what they need to move forward.

Having impressive dashboards is not the goal. Instead, doing better demands that you have a clear-minded appetite for the truth. Armed with the facts, at every point you can make choices and decisions to ensure forward momentum. As a leader, you will model behavior that increases safety and trust so your people feel supported when they have bring any uncomfortable truths to your attention.

As discussed in Chapter 11: "OKRs at Scale," if you're using the localization model I advocate for, you may not need a specialty tracking platform to keep the status of your OKRs and OKR-aligned initiatives status up to date. But if your organization meets the criteria discussed in that chapter, only then is when I recommend considering a specialty platform.

WATCH OUT: STARTING WITH AN OKR PLATFORM TOO EARLY

Many organizations start their OKR implementation by purchasing a specialty OKR platform and then relying on the platform's OKR onboarding and training to achieve methodology adoption.

Some of the most talented OKR professionals in the field sit within those platform client service and training departments (including many dear friends and former colleagues who I think the world of). But unavoidably, platform onboarding is designed to ensure maximum utilization of the platform itself (a key success metric in the field is often weekly active usage), not directly successful adoption and proliferation of the OKR methodology in the way that uniquely suits your organization.

Despite huge investment, a lot of my clients wind up calling me after spending a year working with an OKR platform to implement OKRs and share a similar story.

1. Very few people are using the OKR platform.
2. The organization hasn't learned the OKR methodology in any meaningful way.
3. People who have to put data into the system resent having to dual-enter their data since typically it lives in a delivery planning system and then has to be transferred into the OKR platform.
4. On balance, the cost of the platform is too high for the benefits.

Does this make me anti-OKR platforms? Absolutely not. The typical trajectory for my clients is to work with me to firmly establish their OKR methodology, learning, and behaviors, and then to either employ a system already in their business stack (e.g., Asana, AirTable, Smartsheet, Monday.com, ClickUp, or numerous other common business tools that have OKR functionality) or adopt a purpose-built OKR platform (like Microsoft Viva Goals, WorkBoard, Quantive, or Tability).[64]

OKR platforms implemented well and at the right time can bring your OKR implementation to life. The smart ones allow for:

---

[64] This is an extremely truncated list, including only the platforms I myself have worked with or evaluated for my own business use here. For a long time, I stayed entirely out of the platform conversation to honor a legal obligation to do so; I've only recently begun evaluating platforms again given that I have so many clients asking for trusted referrals. G2.com, a popular online software review site, currently lists 145 tools under its "objectives and key results" category, the vast majority of which even I have never heard of.

1. Coherent goal setting from Level 1 down through the organization, including management of visibility of Initiative progress.

2. Feature reminders, notifications, and prompts, saving your core team avoidable manual labor and the frustrating role of nagging people for their participation.

3. Historical data in a system from past quarters (say, for the ability to rotate key results each quarter year over year).

4. Check-ins on goals; many include feedback and recognition functionality.

5. Drag-and-drop or automated dashboard creation in some tools.

6. Sophisticated analytics on the backend for metrics including usage (and other surveillance data if you're interested) in some tools.

I am not a platform specialist, but I do keep current a list of platforms that I've either tested personally or, employ friends and former colleagues, which you can visit at findrc.co/okrplatforms.

ESTABLISHING YOUR RHYTHM OF BUSINESS

More important than specialty software is the most overlooked element of OKR adoption: changing your organization's behavior from what it is today to what it needs to be to achieve your goals. The lens to view this change through is your business's rhythm of business.

First, let's get familiar with a healthy No-BS OKR cycle.

The No-BS OKR cycle

The No-BS OKR cycle begins in the prior year with a company-level retrospective and reset yielding updates to the strategic stack (and any other of their durable strategic artifacts), as well as creating fresh organizational OKRs for the upcoming year. Senior leadership preliminarily identifies the major initiatives that align to support Level 1/Level 2 OKRs so that they can complete an initial alignment review for alignment and completeness.

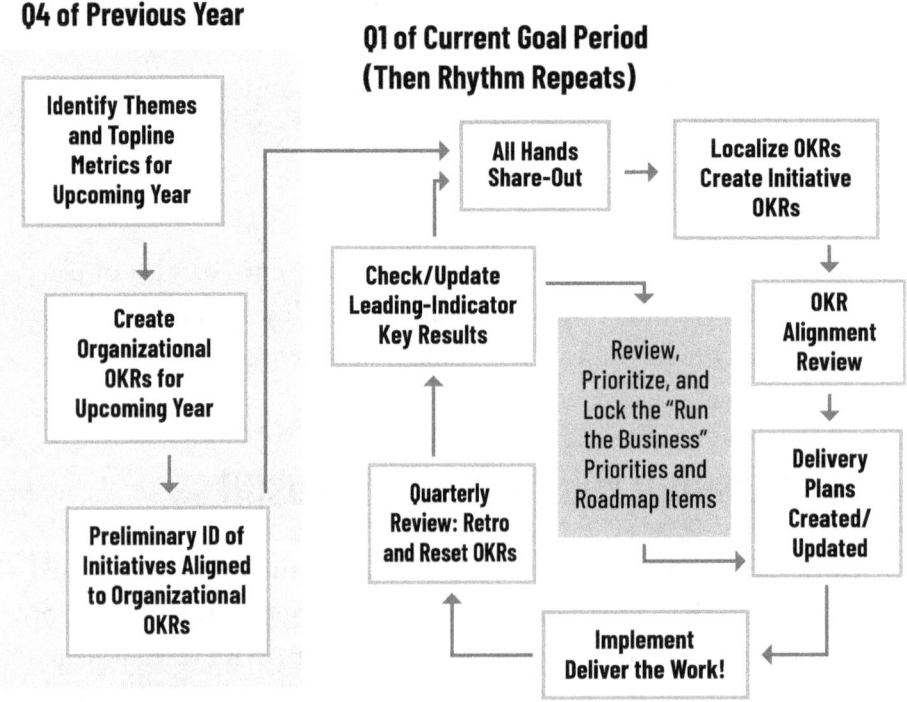

The Level 1 OKRs are shared at an all-hands meeting (with Level 2 leaders sharing their Level 2 OKRs in functional meetings as a fast-follow). Then, the OKR rhythm shifts from top-down to bottom-up; teams and individuals create their goals and plans to align up to the Level 1/Level 2 OKRs. An alignment review should be completed by each Level 2 leader to ensure proper alignment with the rest of the company.

There is a parallel rhythm taking place around the organization's run-the-business priorities and roadmap items. Those items, as we've discussed, may not all be included in OKR conversations, but those plans should be reviewed and refreshed when you know your organizational OKRs to ensure that activities no longer strategically aligned are reduced or stopped.

At this point, it's time to plan your delivery (as efficiently as possible) and then get to work to deliver on your goals. At the end of the goal cycle, there is a review looking back to see what you've learned and looking forward to reset any goals that may be going in the wrong direction.

If you're reading that and thinking, "It would take my company six months to do all that," you're not wrong. Some companies do get trapped in planning paralysis. Back in the days when I didn't have the freedom to exit client engagements, I once spent months working with a client trying to guide them through creation of their OKRs. Just when we seemed close to alignment, they'd recognize that due to the delays some circumstance had changed, requiring an objective or key result to be reworked. The effort was absolutely futile. By the end of nearly two quarters of effort, not only had we lost that time we could have been implementing, it was now time to begin the process again for the future year—at which point I gracefully bowed out.

Here's what the cadence can look like, in a well-organized organization that has developed their No-BS mindset:

- Level 1/Level 2 leaders complete year-end preparation during the last quarter of the preceding year, including performing a retrospective or learning review, updating the company-level strategy if necessary, and creating company-level OKRs.

- The all-hands share-out and Level 2 functional share-outs happen as close to the start of the new year as possible.

- Teams create localized OKRs, initiative OKRs, individual goals, and delivery plans within the first month of the year.

- By the first day of the second month of the year, the organization is moving into implementation.

- The retrospective and reset and updates to any Level 1/ Level 2 OKRs are typically locked during the last two weeks of the period (or the first week of the upcoming period, at the latest).

- The localization, team alignment, and delivery plan updates are much quicker in the repeating cycles, ideally being completed by the end of the second week of the new period to allow as much time as possible focused on implementation.

OKRs traditionally start on an annual/quarterly cadence, which works well for a lot of organizations. Larger organizations with multiple layers that have to complete all of the above may benefit from stretching out their goal cycle a bit. Increasingly, large organizations are shifting to a trimester basis for OKRs (which can work excellently if data availability isn't strictly limited to quarters) or a half-year basis (which trades off some urgency during Q1 and Q3 for longer periods of focus on implementation between goal resets).

There is no universal "right answer" on cadence. Pick a place to start experimenting, see what you learn, and then adapt from there.

Let's take a look at each step in that rhythm in a little more detail.

Year-end retrospective and reset

At the end of the prior year, there is a full company-level retrospective and reset.

There is abundant controversy about whether OKRs or annual operating plans (which includes budgets) should come first; OKRs and budget are both chickens and eggs. The idealist in me wants to say they should be developed in parallel, but I've seen the annual operating plan process in large organizations. The people responsible for the annual plan can do no more than they are already doing during budget season. So realistically, despite the chicken-and-egg problems it may cause, I see most organizations setting their budget first and then fast-following with a time-compressed OKR creation cycle.

Does it make sense to align on your stretch priorities before you lock a budget? Sure. That would set your stretch efforts up for success.

Would doing so introduce all sorts of unknowable unknowns into your budget considerations? Yes, absolutely.

The best advice I can give is to create your annual operating plan based on your run-the-business knowledge with some padding to support known stretch priorities. Consider your budget the imperfect forecast it is, then create your OKRs and make budget adjustments if necessary.

With your annual operating plan in hand, refresh your memory about your strategic priorities and brush up or create your strategic stack, your company-level OKRs, and Level 2 OKRs (by Level 2 leaders), and ideally, perform a preliminary identification of initiatives aligned to organizational OKRs and complete an alignment review (described in more detail below).

This gets the organization ready for the transparency of sharing the candidate OKRs with the entire organization.

Communicating OKRs to the organization

It's best practice for organizational OKRs to be communicated to the organization through a town-hall session or an all-hands meeting. Leaders can share the organizational objectives and key results as well as clarifying descriptions or information that gives the OKRs important context.

The other purpose of the announcement of the OKRs, in addition to socializing that they exist, is giving the team members a chance to ask questions about what they contain. Ideally the OKRs have been pre-socialized with important stakeholders so there shouldn't be any large surprises by the time of the town hall or all-hands meeting. But we don't live in an ideal world, so the all-hands meeting should feature OKRs that are complete to the stage of "soft Jello": they're not so rough draft that they show the leadership team having a lack of clarity or confidence in their vision or direction, but they're not so final that if you discover something important during the all-hands socialization you can't change them.

Announcing objectives and key results through the all-hands (then following up by sending them out in writing or sharing a draft version for deeper review and feedback) gives the organization at large an understanding of both your shared purpose and your shared responsibilities, important context to maximize the chance that you'll achieve your OKRs, and a chance to highlight any big misses or issues as a final quality control check.

In a low-fidelity, lightweight model, the following artifacts assist in communicating (and tracking) OKRs:

- At Level 1: a slide or presentation version (for all-hands and as a one-sheet to keep front and center) and a tracker version (a spreadsheet or dashboard).

- At Level 2: a slide or presentation version (again, so you can see the OKRs for your organization at a glance) and a tracker version (usually linked to or part of the Level 1 tracking spreadsheet or dashboard).

- At Level 3+: team and initiative OKRs may be presented on slides, but often they're also written into a team or initiative charter or operating document so they're somewhere central that stays top of mind.

Tracking is often distributed and highly variable at Level 3+ of the organization, since different teams often have different existing delivery planning and management software and systems. What's important is that each team or initiative has *one* single source of truth document with status and progress information that's in a known location that can be linked to from the Level 1/Level 2 tracking spreadsheet or dashboard. If there are key results at Level 3+ that roll up to the Level 1 or Level 2 key results mathematically, that can be built into the Level 1/Level 2 system (or this is where an OKR platform may be considered).

Localizing objectives and key results

After the all-hands meeting, Level 2 leaders share their Level 2 OKRs locally, and then OKRs can be localized through the organization. As was discussed in Chapter 11: "OKRs at Scale," in the No-BS OKR model we don't recommend using the structured cascading approach advocated by some earlier OKR implementation guidance. Instead, during the localization stage, teams may look up at the organizational OKRs

> **What's important is that each team or initiative has one single source of truth.**

and identify what important progress indicators and outcome measures their work will contribute to the upline OKRs.

Typically most organizations do individual goal setting on an annual or twice-yearly cycle. When the year's objectives and key results are announced to the organization at large, after team and initiative OKRs are created individuals can look up at the organizational, team, and initiative OKR to which they align, to inform their individual goal setting, per the practices discussed in Chapter 13: "Aligned Individual Goals."

Aligning OKRs via an alignment review

Again, alignment is an important step that many organizations fail to take. Organizations burn so much time creating OKRs that by the time the OKRs are written the team is perfectly happy to put them in a slide deck and forget they exist. Instead, what's transformative about your draft OKRs is evaluating your completed system of OKRs at the organizational, team, and initiative levels with a comprehensive review to ensure alignment.

Alignment is another step in the process that sells OKR specialty software. Even I, as an advocate for using standard business tools for OKR tracking, must admit that a full alignment review with more than two levels of OKRs is often overwhelming (or may prove impossible) for organizations without using some sort of OKR specialty platform or software solution. (It may be overwhelming even with software, for what it's worth.)

The way I was originally trained to complete an alignment review is to convene a large meeting with major stakeholders. I'd deliver the full set of OKRs in some single view prior to the meeting with a request that participants review, note their alignment issue spots, and come prepared to discuss and resolve any alignment collisions.

However, alignment reviews operated that way don't work. The closest I've come is to see leaders fully align one or two OKRs and then decide the rest are good enough and call it a day. This isn't usually a bad outcome, but it leaves people feeling like their work is unfinished.

The point is, even if the OKRs are focused and intentionally aligned, the volume in most organizations is so large that doing an alignment review just feels overwhelming. I've tried a number of tooling approaches to solve this. I've built linked spreadsheet ecosystems so leaders can explore an entire set of OKRs; I've used OKR platform full-alignment functionality. But no matter the delivery mechanism, in the real world, the conventional approach to full alignment review is just too much for most organizations.

It doesn't have to be this way. By incorporating No-BS OKR practices and creating OKRs that are aligned from the start, your alignment reviews will be more doable.

- Limit the number of objects in your full system of OKRs.
- Align OKRs as they are developed through collaborative review and discussion during drafting; don't develop them in silos and then reconcile.
- Conduct the alignment review meeting as focused, brief, and limited to only a few people: a senior leader, and chief of staff or right hand, or operating officer to look across the entire system of OKRs.
- Resolve alignment issues through sidebar conversations with only the affected parties.

It's not necessary to re-announce the OKRs via an additional all-hands after the alignment review unless there are significant material changes at the company level. Even in that case, updating the organization could be done with written communication. People will see the finished, aligned OKRs when they're delivered for localization and can adapt to any changes made during alignment review at that time.

Once your OKRs are created, localized, and aligned, it's time to achieve them.

The implementation phase

A Learning and Performance-Focused Periodic Cycle

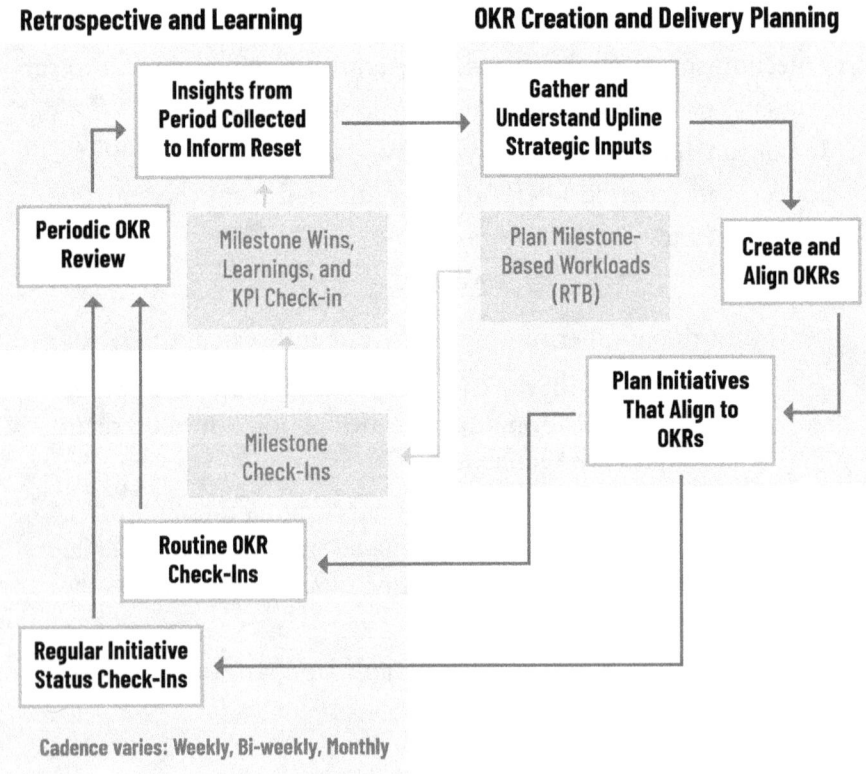

Retrospective and Learning

OKR Creation and Delivery Planning

Insights from Period Collected to Inform Reset

Gather and Understand Upline Strategic Inputs

Periodic OKR Review

Milestone Wins, Learnings, and KPI Check-in

Plan Milestone-Based Workloads (RTB)

Create and Align OKRs

Plan Initiatives That Align to OKRs

Milestone Check-Ins

Routine OKR Check-Ins

Regular Initiative Status Check-Ins

Cadence varies: Weekly, Bi-weekly, Monthly

Implementation

During the implementation phase, what's most important is that teams have an intentional division of time between their run-the-business activities—typically planned based on milestones—and their initiatives and efforts supporting OKR achievement. Teams that carry a heavy growth, innovation, and transformation burden may spend the majority of their time on OKR-aligned workloads or activities with little run-the-business time being spent. Teams that have a heavy operational burden may spend the majority of their time on run-the-business-aligned workloads or activities with a small slice of their time spent dedicated to improving an inefficient process or practice with a single OKR around operational improvement.

Both types of work must be recognized as important. Workloads that align to your OKRs may include your most important growth transformation and innovation initiatives, but it's not fair to the teams that carry a heavy run-the-business burden to say that only the OKRs reflect what's most important in the business. Keeping the lights on, keeping the bills paid, and all the many rhythms that keep a business operating are also critical. During the implementation phase, attention should be paid to run-the-business progress as well as to OKRs through status and risk assessment conversations.

Status and risk assessment meetings

There's a tendency in organizations to avoid bad news. No-BS OKRs challenge that tendency head on. When you transition into the implementation phase, your job is to remain clear-eyed about your progress. Rather than gathering for status reporting meetings about activities, No-BS OKR organizations restructure their schedules so that status and risk reporting meetings encompass both run-the-business and OKR-aligned workloads.

But the purpose of these meetings is not merely to talk about how much work you've been doing (or how well it's going). Outcomes matter. When you gather, it's appropriate to celebrate your wins, to recognize your progress, and also to be honest about risks to achievement that you face.

To overcome the cognitive biases that encourage you to report the good news and hide the bad news, you must work at it consciously. Implementation-phase meeting agendas should provide time for recognition of progress and new knowledge, time for identification of risks and roadblocks, and time for problem-solving—and communicating unmet needs—in order to keep the work on track.

> **To overcome biases that encourage reporting good news and hiding the bad, you must work at it consciously.**

In the beginning of this rhythm, often many teams tackle the first item on the agenda—the sharing of good news—and take the entire allotted time to do so to avoid raising risks and roadblocks. The answer is not longer meetings; the answer is to be more judicious about what is shared in terms of good news and the wins. Every completed item doesn't necessarily need to be reported. Leaders should share their wins, failures, and what they learned transparently, modeling the intellectual humility they need from their teams. Focus the sharing of wins on new knowledge that can be applied broadly.

It may take teams time to develop the trust to share bad news in meetings, so it's important that early experimenters are supported when they do so.

Collaboration sessions

Another feature of No-BS OKR implementation is instead of raising risks and roadblocks only at status meetings, periodic collaboration sessions are scheduled to address them.

Sometimes risks and roadblocks need to be cleared by an executive sponsor or stakeholder. But when an issue is more complicated, a collaboration session with the key stakeholders creates an environment for shared problem-solving. OKRs describe shared responsibilities, so even if an OKR has an owner or is more the responsibility of one person compared to others, it's important that no one is struggling or suffering in OKRs alone.

Learning reviews and OKR resets

Over the course of a quarter, year, or other implementation phase, don't only pursue achievement of your OKRs but also be inquisitive about what you learn through your experiments with OKRs. Few people or teams create ideal, maximally impactful objectives and key results in their first cycle; you'll learn how to create more powerful objectives and key results by creating your first key results, working toward them, and intentionally reviewing what you learn and seeing how you can improve for future cycles.

Almost every OKR rhythm includes some type of quarterly OKR retrospective and reset, often treated as one and the same thing. Teams are coached to prepare beforehand by capturing their insights about the past goal cycle with any number of typical retrospective formats. (Start/Stop/Continue is a common one; Wins/Losses/Learnings is another I've seen utilized; and you can see my ecosystem-style Learning Review example below.) Then, meet to re-examine the OKRs from the last cycle and make any updates necessary—the OKR "reset." In most OKR reset approaches:

- Any achieved objectives or key results are retired.
- Any new necessary objectives or key results are added.

Generally, that approach works if people actually participate, although I frequently see teams get bogged down in discussion of the operations of their OKR rhythm during the retrospective component instead of really focusing on and discussing their OKR progress and performance itself.

I prefer to think of the retrospective and the reset as two distinct phases that are both focused on the substantive OKRs themselves: a learning review, which focuses first on reviewing progress and performance on the last goal period's OKRs to capture as many new insights as possible about the substance of the OKRs; and then the reset. This keeps the full focus on the substance of the OKRs themselves. Then after that, an operational huddle can be convened (e.g., some teams, after resetting OKRs for the upcoming cycle, do a quick feedback survey specific to the OKR operations).

After looking at objective and key results status and progress and exploring the reasons behind the performance (whether high, low, or non-existent), I use the following retrospective questions[65]:

1. **What goes in the burn pile?**
   What are you moving on from entirely because it's out-dated, no longer serves you, or doesn't contribute to your future in any way? Where do you have invasive weeds that just need to go? That are no longer good for you, your business, or your people?

2. **What goes in the compost?**
   What did you try that died on the vine or that didn't work but is worth trying again? What should you keep or con-tinue but needs to take a new form to be useful?

[65]   I keep an excerpt from the No-BS OKRs Workbook on the Learning Review rhythm available for free on my website at findrc.co/OKRReset.

3. **What are your cultivation opportunities?**
   What seeds did you plant that need help to grow? What seeds would you like to plant next? When you envision your "garden" at the end of this OKR cycle, what's different?

Objectives often span more than one quarter and sometimes more than one year; leading indicator or progress key results may repeat or shift from quarter to quarter. In most systems of OKRs, however, a periodic review and reset (quarterly, trimesterly, or annually) ensures that OKRs stay relevant and keep you pointed in the right direction.

Don't forget to employ an intentional continuous learning approach to improving the OKRs themselves. Most approaches to implementing OKRs lump learning reviews and resets together. The end-of-quarter rhythm item might even be called a "retrospective and reset." But even if both functions happen in the same meeting, there are two distinct parts:

1. Taking stock of what you've learned (retrospective).
2. Deciding how your goals, plans, and operations may change based on that new knowledge (reset).

OKR quarterly reviews can quickly become a laundry list of frustrations with OKRs themselves. Just like arguing about the difference between an objective and a goal to avoid the discomfort of creating and committing to OKRs, quarterly reviews can be an exercise in avoiding the discomfort of learning and failures by redirecting attention to the OKR core team and their OKR implementation. Don't let this happen. Some organizations separate the conversations by conducting their OKR reset, where the substance of the OKR progress (attainment) is reviewed and the goals themselves reset if need be, followed by a separate touch-base on OKR methodology and operational improvement.

Case study: Quarterly business review revamp

A large division within an enterprise organization needed to improve their ROI on OKR time spent; their quarterly business review was a recognized pain point. While senior leaders liked getting so much information in one sitting, everyone else found the meeting painful. It took time to prep; the "meeting" itself involved three sessions, each lasting one or two hours, with up to 77 people on each invitation.

My conservative calculations for only the cost of attendance put this at $40K for what was largely a marathon rapid-fire status report, with a lot of subjective opinion, spin, and a little substance.

The OKR core team, senior leaders, and I worked together on a revised approach that included:

1. **Eliminating milestones from the OKRs.** Milestones were already accounted for in the organization's delivery plans (covered in another standing meeting). There was no reason to repeat them in the OKR quarterly business review. By removing them, we significantly reduced the total number of items that were up for consideration for discussion.

2. **Providing specific expectations for changed behavior to presenters and senior leaders.** Presenters were expected to only discuss actual objectives and key results and to prioritize truth over accomplishment, leaving time to highlight setbacks, new knowledge, and blockers that needed assistance to clear. Leaders were reminded not to punish or dwell on fault around setbacks or mistakes; instead, they should to focus constructively with team members on how to remove roadblocks and move forward.

The new system didn't erase accountability—managers and the organization's delivery plans would still hold teams to their milestones.

But the shift from reporting to problem-solving freed up time for meaningful discussion of what was most important. The new behaviors everyone put into practice increased psychological safety for sharing the bad news as well as the good so that everyone could work together to move at-risk key results into the green.

In the first quarterly review using the new approach, the client's results were impressive. Total meeting time was cut 75%, from four hours to one. The number of topics were cut by 60%, which meant more time to discuss what was most important, even with a shorter meeting. Conversations focused on obstacles and needs, leveraging leadership's ability to support and problem solve.

Quarterly reviews became more of a discussion than a report, so participants left the meeting with a clear path forward.

What a rhythm of business for goal achievement looks like

What's the best way to communicate your rhythm of business? You won't be surprised to hear me answer: on a single page.

The example below shows a rhythm of business that takes into account internal and external touchpoints and what happens daily, weekly, bi-weekly, monthly, quarterly, and annually.

Now, before you object that your organization can't afford to add on a whole new process for OKRs or invest the time and energy in creating a formal rhythm of business, that's not at all what I'm advocating. Your organization already has a rhythm of business, whether you've written it down or not. How do I know this? Because your rhythm of business is your culture—not a process.

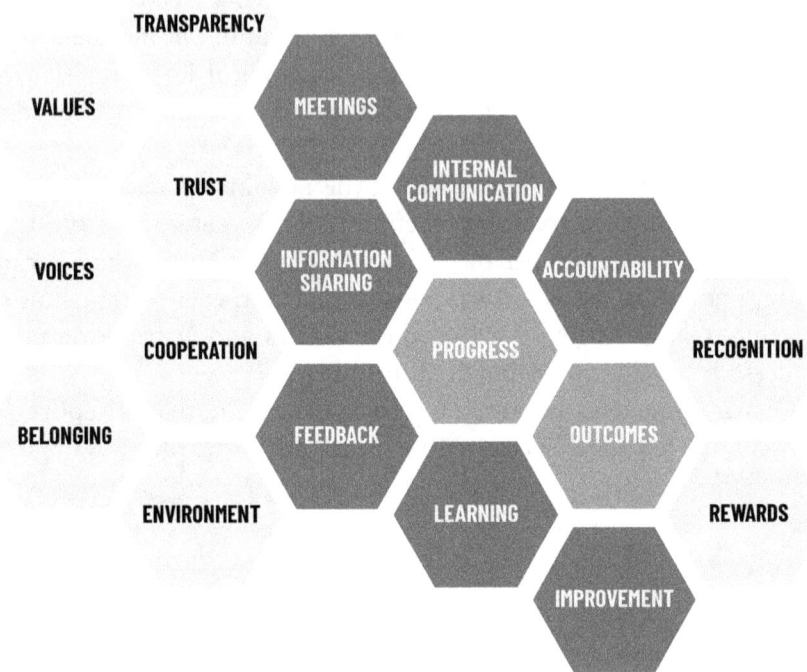

There are already recurring meetings, cadences, rituals; there are dates that carry internal and external expectations. What I'm suggesting is that you take note of the rhythm of business your organization is already executing and then determine both what's missing and where in your existing rhythm you can make shifts to increase goal attainment and continuous learning.

A rhythm of business inventory is one of the most transformative experiences my workshop participants and clients complete. Doing this assessment clarifies whether all the meetings and other rituals already in place are achieving what they hope they are.

EXERCISE: ASSESS AND DOCUMENT YOUR RHYTHM OF BUSINESS FOR GOAL ACHIEVEMENT

Step 1: Assessment questions

To complete a rhythm of business assessment, begin by asking yourself three questions:

1. What's working about your rhythm of business today?
2. What's most important to improve in your rhythm of business?
3. Is there anything you need to stop doing to make your rhythm of business more efficient and impactful?

Step 2: Complete inventory

With those answers in hand, next complete an inventory:

1. What are your organization's mandatories (whether they exist today or not) in terms of meetings, communication rhythms, routines/rituals?
2. What synchronous and asynchronous communication rhythms make the most sense for your team?
3. What meetings (with what durations, frequencies, and purposes) make the most sense for your team?
4. What accountability measures ensure that commitments are kept and blockers cleared?
5. At which specific points in your meetings or communication rhythms will your progress be examined to identify and address blockers and new knowledge?

6. Where in your rhythm of business do you take time to specifically focus on your OKRs, and other important but perhaps not-urgent matters?

Be sure you consider both internal and external stakeholders when answering those questions.

Step 3: Design your rhythm of business

Now: get out your sticky notes and a big sheet of paper or a white-board, and design an improved and intentional rhythm of business on a single page.

Here's how I set up the page:

Daily	Weekly	Bi-weekly	Monthly	Quarterly	Half-Year/Annually
Internal					
External					

Place your mandatories, communication rhythms, meetings, and accountability measures on that map, making sure that ultimately it fits to a single page (or screen). I like to use a little graduation hat icon to indicate which meetings are specifically focused on learning and a little bullseye to indicate which meetings will include a focus on OKRs.

It may take a few iterations before your rhythm of business is really working well, but that effort is very much worth it. It's surprising how many meetings serve little or no purpose; how much meeting and communication time is spent on status reporting; and how little time an organization spends focused on learning from setbacks and clearing blockers.

> **It's surprising how little time an organization spends focused on learning from setbacks and clearing blockers.**

Whatever you find, your organization will benefit greatly from an intentional rhythm of business, as opposed to an ad-hoc one.

TL^DR: STRATEGIST TAKEAWAYS

- Creating OKRs is only the first step: operationalizing them is how you achieve their promise.

- Operationalizing OKRs is not just about tracking: it's about identifying how in your rhythm of business you can implement practices to succeed on your OKRs.

- More important than OKR systems and software are the behaviors and habits you rely on to uncover the truth of your progress and achievement.

- Instead of only recognizing and rewarding heroism, organizations can recognize and reward incidents of courage or ambition that yield important new knowledge; incidents of important failures (because a lot is learned in failure); as well as wins.

- If you think you don't have a rhythm of business, you do. Take the time to write it down, and make sure it's designed for goal achievement.

16

CONGRATULATIONS, YOU STRATEGIST, YOU!

That's it! You've made it. You got through the mental shifts of Part 1, learned how to create OKRs in Part 2, and read whichever parts of the advanced learning topics in Part 3 are relevant to your role and situation. All that's left is for you to take what you've learned here and apply it in your efforts to change the world for the better.

Believe it or not, this has been the shortest, most useful book on OKRs I could put together to answer the questions I'm routinely asked, after several years of trying. I hope reading and exploring these ideas has been a positive experience in your own OKR learning. Please share your wins and what you've learned with me. Stop by saralobkovich.com anytime or email hello@saralobkovich.com with your success stories as well as the things that trip you up.

WHERE TO GO FROM HERE

There are two books I highly recommend for passionate OKR experts who want deeper detail on traditional OKRs, including:

- *Objectives and Key Results* by Paul Niven and Ben Lamorte. I consider this to be the definitive treatise on OKRs.

- *OKRs Field Guide* by Ben Lamorte: a remarkably practical and useful book for OKR coaches and champions, which is a great "getting started" guide for new and experienced OKR coaches.

I keep a list of recommended reading on my website at findrc.co/book-club, including those two books and more.

I eye content created by the OKR platforms skeptically because their focus isn't always on methodological excellence, but it's inarguable that much of the world's strongest OKR expertise is centralized within the platforms' client service and support departments. Remember that OKR platforms are trying to sell you software when consuming their content, but as long as you keep that in mind and maintain your focus on implementing a coherent, well-thought-out methodological approach to OKRs instead of a software-first one, OKR platform resources can provide invaluable learning.

I share deeper dives on many of the topics I covered more lightly here via my blogs and podcast:

1. The No-BS OKRs blog lives at findrc.co/nobsokrsblog. There, you'll find all of my free, public, No-BS OKR-related content, including a series of OKR FAQs I update regularly (so please let me know what I've missed).

2. My podcast, *Thinkydoers*, is where you'll find audio versions of much of my No-BS OKRs information. Also there are tools, resources, and support for status quo challengers, as well as inspirational stories and practice tips from fascinating people whose work spans thinking (strategy) and doing (execution).

If you would like information about how to work with me:

1. Information about my coaching and learning and development work with organizations is online at findrc.co/workwithsara.

2. Information about my 1:1 and group programs supporting individuals with their career fulfillment is available at findrc.co/icoaching.

3. I host a membership called Unblock Your Inner Strategist for year-round support creating and achieving your most important goals. For more information, visit: findrc.co/ubyis.

4. My favorite thing in the whole world to do is to train and enable OKR coaches. For information about training to become a No-BS OKR Coach and part of the No-BS OKR Coach roster, please visit findrc.co/okrcoachtrain.

The larger OKR professional community is a large, welcoming, engaged, and highly collaborative environment to work within, and I feel very lucky to be a part of such a creative and passionate community. I keep a list of partners, communities, and other connection points in the space on my website at findrc.co/partners.

WHAT I HOPE YOU REMEMBER

This has been a very long read. Now that you're at the very end, here's what I hope you've learned and remember.

For far too long, the field of strategy has been an ivory tower, accessible only to people who satisfied some criteria I'll never really understand—I just knew it wasn't me. I never had the right companies or schools on my resume. What I had was a strategically wired brain. It took me a long time to figure that out, to provide that brain the tools and working conditions my brain needed to do its best work, and to find the community of strategic rebels I now so respect and admire whose work has helped me find my own place in the field.

And in that process, here's what I've learned. Strategists are the people who look around and see how things can be better. We're wired to observe people and the world around us: facts and observations are the essential ingredients of strategic insight, and for many of us, it's our effort to understand and be understood by others that propels us in this work with so much passion and determination.

You, my friend, have always had an inner strategist. Maybe you haven't had the tools or the confidence to let those skills shine, but they are there, just waiting to be awakened. Now that you've gotten acquainted with your own inner strategist, I hope you are energized to translate your vision for change into reality.

The world needs your unique perspective, your audacious goals, and your relentless persistence to make things better. Whether you're transforming a Fortune 100 company, starting a community initiative, or putting what you've learned to work to build your own career fulfillment, your strategic thinking and doing will create ripples of change that reach far beyond what you can see.

So please: Go forth, you brilliant strategist, you. Challenge the status quo (with solutions). Lead the charge into uncharted territory (because that's what the future is). Create your own strategic One-Sheet to keep visible to guide yourself and your work; build your own No-BS OKRs quickly and start learning. Because every big thing that's ever gotten done started with someone like you saying, "What if?"

You, my friend, are a strategist. The future is waiting. And I can't wait to see what you create.

GLOSSARY

Aligned individual goals: Goals created by individuals that are aligned to upline group or shared objectives and key results. Aligned individual goals blend individual intrinsic interest and motivation with the needs of the organization to create benefits for both.

Alignment: When strategic coordination within an organization ensures collaborators are working effectively toward common goals. When employees' actions and systems are congruent with the organization's strategic progress, demonstrating unity of purpose. When resources and activities are optimized and coordinated, to increase organizational productivity. When the organization works harmoniously, without unnecessary collisions or conflict, as much as possible.

Alignment layer: The alignment layer sits between the durable strategic artifacts and delivery planning mechanisms to make sure that there is signal on progress and risks while working and that there is clarity and agreement about the most important criteria for success. It contains objective and key results as well as identification of important key performance indicators, and sometimes also includes major milestones or other mandatory goals.

Annual operating plan: A document that makes up many organization's "strategy" at the top of strategic stack; it may be an actual strategy but is often an annual budget.

Baseline key result: A key result meant to instrument and identify a starting value for a metric or measure the business hasn't previously tracked. Often written in the form: "Build and instrument a model to measure [metric] and baseline its [increase/decrease/improvement]."

Business as usual: See Run-the-business.

Cascading: The idea of cascading or localizing OKRs is to connect the dots between strategy and execution in a theoretically clear, aligned way. The idea is to start with organizational OKRs at the company-level or top of the organization, and then sequentially cascade them down through the layers of the organization into the domain of each suborganization, subteam, and even person in some implementations. To my knowledge, this concept gained steam based on the focus on cascading in *Measure What Matters*. See also: Connecting OKRs and Localization.

Changemaker: An individual or entity that drives social and organizational transformation by actively pursuing innovation and actions that create positive and sustainable impact. Changemakers are typically thinkers and doers, not afraid to challenge the status quo and rally others to join their cause to create a better future.

Connecting OKRs: "Creating sets of OKRs throughout the company that align with your highest-level OKRs . . . and signal the unique contribution offered from teams and individuals throughout the enterprise" (from *Objectives and Key Results* by Paul Niven and Ben Lamorte, page 99). See also: Cascading and Localization; all three are related terms.

Delivery plan: Project plans and task management that attempt to capture and communicate the organization's planned activities, deadlines, and project status.

Failure: When an experiment doesn't go according to plan and the desired result does not occur. An important step in learning and change.

Fidelity: High-fidelity describes a design that is detailed and closely resembles a final product. Low-fidelity describes a design that is simpler and less detailed. Low-fidelity prototypes and designs are often basic and used in the early stages of idea development to quickly test ideas and concepts. They may be simple sketches or wireframes with little detail. High-fidelity design work encourages critical review (or approval based on appearance, not necessarily substance if the work is "beautiful"); low-fidelity work puts the focus on the concepts involved and encourages creative and collaborative feedback.

Functional organization: The major disciplines that are often represented in most companies, including HR, Operations, Product, Marketing, Sales, Customer Support, Information Technology, etc.

Goal: The object or aim of an action. A statement of aspirational change that contributes to high performance by increasing motivation, knowledge and skill development, effort, persistence, and development of knowledge and task strategy. An experiment in how to improve or do better.

Index measures/index key results: Like the S&P 500 Index in the stock market, an experimental index key result may be built by assembling a number of available contributing facts or quantifiable observations, weighting each, and calculating a single numerical "score" or index. Indexes may take some experimentation to validate, so don't trust that a new index experiment is giving you good data—but over the course of a couple of quarters, you can iterate and adjust the inputs and weighting until you're getting useful information from the index calculation.

Initiative: An initiative is a named workload or body of work that describes how one or more OKRs will be achieved. Initiatives are the workloads that align up to the achievement of OKRs. They may be functional or cross-functional, and can sit at different levels of the organization depending on their importance.

Key performance indicators (KPIs): Business metrics being tracked to make sure the business is healthy and headed in the right direction. If an organization had a human body, its blood pressure, pulse, and cholesterol levels might be KPIs; they're the metrics you keep an eye on to make sure the business stays healthy.

Key result: Empirically measurable stretch goals that align to objectives and describe how the organization quantifies progress and success for the sake of achieving its most important outcomes (and learning and improving for the future). They are singular in focus. Key results are presumed to be stretch goals unless they are clearly labeled as a mandatory goal.

Lagging indicator: A downstream metric or measure that ultimately changes as a result of the activities you undertake toward achieving your outcome. Lagging indicators reflect results; they don't predict results.

Leading indicator: An upstream metric or measure that provides early signal about the progress of your activities. Leading indicators predict results and help guide actions to achieve desired outcomes. Because they're predictive and proactive, leading indicators enable you to make adjustments before final results are determined.

Level 1/Level 2/Level 3 OKRs: Level 1 OKRs typically sit at the company level and are typically highly cross-functional. Level 1.5 OKRs may reflect OKRs created for regions or divisions within a large global enterprise that are themselves "company-like." Level 2 OKRs are typically a mix of mostly functional and some cross-functional goals, and focus on each function localizing the Level 1/1.5 OKRs into their domain. Level 2 cross-functional OKRs, when present, reflect the localization of Level 1 OKRs into high-level collaborative teams usually sitting at senior levels of the organization. Level 3 OKRs (in all but the largest organizations) reflect the localization to teams and/or for initiatives that are typically "locally managed" by a team.

Localization: The idea of cascading or localizing OKRs is to connect the dots between strategy and execution in a theoretically clear, aligned way. The idea is to start with organizational OKRs at the company level or top of the organization, and then sequentially localize them down through the layers of the organization by contextualizing them for the domain of each suborganization and subteam See also: Connecting OKRs, Cascading.

Mandatory goal: A mandatory, 100% must-achieve goal or target, on which the organization is not safe to fail. There may be consequences for non-achievement; therefore, the organization must prioritize and support mandatory goals with the needed budget and resources.

Milestone: An important event or stage in the creation or development process, typically stated in the structure of "Complete [activity] by [date]."

Minimum viable product (MVP): The simplest possible version of a product or deliverable that can be released to the market to test product/market fit or to gather new knowledge from users without the overhead and investment of building a finished product. The purpose of an MVP is to develop just enough to test product/market-fit and to be usable enough that users can test and provide feedback for future development.

Mission: A statement that describes the activity of an organization in the context of the organization's vision. An organization's mission statement further assists customers in understanding what to expect in terms of what the organization does in the world.

No-BS OKRs: A straightforward, simple approach to creating and achieving objectives and key results (OKRs) made up of two parts: 1) clear, visionary, directional objectives, and 2) empirically measurable key results: progress and outcome targets that align on what success means and reveal whether you're on or off track.

North Star metric: The most important (typically non-financial) measure of an organization's success or impact; when that metric is healthy and growing, the organization is healthy and growing.

Objective: Aspirational, inspired, directional statements of intent that describe what's most important and why it matters for the goal term. Objectives are qualitative, inspirational, and action-oriented. They are designed to align the organization around a shared purpose and provide clarity on what success means.

Objectives and Key Results (OKRs): Objectives and Key Results are a method for collaborative goal setting and organizational alignment that derived from Peter Drucker's Management by Objectives (MBO); OKRs gained widespread awareness thanks to John Doerr's 2018 book *Measure What Matters*.

Outcome: Something, according to Merriam-Webster Dictionary, "that follows as a result or consequence." Outcomes are not outputs (activities); outcomes are the impacts or results that activities yield.

Performance management: The process by which managers and employees work together to plan, monitor, and review employee work objectives and overall contribution, usually for purposes of growth, development, and individual rewards and recognition.

Rebelutionary: A term I coined to describe the workplace rebels and revolutionaries who have the audacity to believe that change is possible and that the risks of sticking with the status quo outweigh the risks of experimenting toward progress.

Rhythm of business: The regular, recurring activities and processes that drive the operations of an organization. Meetings, planning, progress and performance reviews, and communication cadence that keep a business operating.

Run-the-business: All the workloads that keep a business operating, including corporate functions like legal and accounting, and operational maintenance (like maintenance of legacy code in a software development setting). Run-the-business is the essential work that "keeps the lights on" and "keeps the trains operating on time," without which the basic functions of the business would fail to operate.

Target-behavior key results: A key result based on observable behavior, spontaneous feedback, or other information that's able to be counted (even if it's not yet an instrumented business metric).

Territories: A territory, like a theme, is an identifier for a group of concepts that align to each other. For example, when creating key results, you may know that you need a key result in the territory of growth and development, but may not yet know what exactly the metric or key result itself will be.

Textbook key result: A textbook key result is written in the form: "[Increase/decrease/improve] [a metric] by [X%] from [Y] to [Z]." They're called "textbook" because it's quite difficult to write a key result following that formula that isn't a best practice key result.

Themes: A theme, like a territory, is an identifier for a group of concepts that align to each other. For example, when creating objectives, you may know that you need an objective that speaks to financial health. Financial health is a theme.

Thinkydoer: Thinkydoers are people whose work-wiring spans thinking and doing: from insight to idea, through the messy middle, to bring their vision of progress and change to life.

Topline measures: The small number of most-important metrics that show progress or success toward the upline strategic goals; when your toplines are healthy and growing, your North Star is healthy and growing, and your organization is healthy and growing.

Vision: A forward-looking, aspirational statement that outlines an organization's desired future state and the changed future an organization aspires to create. The vision enunciates the organization's reason for being, in terms of its essential purpose. A vision acts as a cornerstone or guiding beacon, to inspire employees, inform decision-making, align stakeholders, and tell customers why the organization exists.

Watermelon metric: A term used to describe the situation where a metric appears to be on track (or is reported subjectively as being on track) or "in the green," on the surface, but which is actually at risk or problematic ("in the red") either when examined more closely or when the ultimate important outcome is not achieved. The precise origin of the term is unknown, but it is used in OKR, business, and project management circles to describe the tendency to report on superficial success while hiding underlying issues.

ACKNOWLEDGMENTS

This book would never have been completed without the support of a small army of people. In fact, I had serious doubts about whether it was even worth finishing the manuscript until I received enthusiastic and helpful feedback from first round beta readers: David Kokorowski, Claire Gordon, Rory Hibbler, and Jeffrey Rhodes. This book is a much better final product thanks to second round beta readers: Wasit Prombutr, Ben Arendt, Jason Johnston, Kris Jennings, Mary Moore, Aaron McKenna, Maggie Mao, Henri Sora, Elie Casamitjana, Kim Ehrman, Claire Gordon, David Hinz, Lou Franco, Joel Benge, Brian Hall, and two anonymous contributors known only as "Vigilant Eagle" and "Advanced Cormorant." Ben and Kris, it was a gift to walk the self-publishing path a few steps behind you both, and I'm so grateful for your friendship. And Andrew Wynne, you may not have been a beta reader, but your support and reminders to take care of myself in the home stretch of this book were greatly appreciated.

This book would not exist without my clients who must mostly remain anonymous due to my confidentiality agreements. An exception must be made for Cindy (White) Shea, Tom ap Simon, Liz Wielinski, Jen Henderson, Marlene Olsavsky, and Kees Bols. I've learned so much working alongside each of you, and am grateful for the inspiration you've provided for me to continuously improve my practices.

Jen Anderson, Amanda B. Nguyen-Axten, Jessi Brown, Sara Hendrickson, Ashley Ball, and Amanda Nicol: thanks to you six, I finally figured out what I want to be when I grow up by watching you work (and how you work), through our creative and strategic collaborations, and friendships.

Brea Starmer and Dr. Renee St. Jacques: I will never forget walking into that big room at Microsoft with you two and facilitating that very first OKR training. My, how far we've come!

Laura Matthews and Caerus Kourt: There were a few times when the only thing that kept this project going was me knowing how much labor and love you've both poured into it. Thank you for your collaboration in bringing this book to life, and helping shape it into what it's become.

Ellie Dela Rosa: Without you and your work, this book would still be a rough draft in a Sharepoint folder (or worse). You've brought so much energy, kindness, and life to this work, and I appreciate you every single day.

Sarah Moon, Kris Jones, Jamar Diggs, and Taliah Good: Thank you for helping me find the confidence to tell the truth and be as "me" as possible in my work. You've helped me find the words I need to reach my people.

Thank you to Lorraine Ferra for putting my words in print all those years ago and to you and my uncle Robert Lingafelter for helping me discover my identity as a "writer."

To my lifelong biggest fan (and I am yours), Megan Ball, and my parents, Dick and Linda Lingafelter: Thank you for helping me believe that the messages of *Free to Be You and Me* apply to me, too, and for supporting me through all the twists and turns of life. To my husband, Chris Lobkovich: Thank you for the daily reminder at my writing desk that each time we make it to the ground, we'll take the next chance together; and for not letting me give up on this project despite the consequences (even if they are "rookie numbers"). I aspire to be the person you believe I am, and that helps me set my bar for living life higher and higher.

ABOUT THE AUTHOR

Sara Lobkovich is a strategist, nationally board-certified health and wellness coach, OKR activist, and host of the *Thinkydoers* podcast. She is the founder and principal consultant at Red Currant Collective, where she enables Rebelutionary leaders and Thinkydoers to achieve their goals and create positive impact. Her 30+ year career (and counting) spans experience in fields including technology, law, marketing, advertising, strategic operations, and organizational learning and change. She has an "other life" in professional motorcycle road racing—for that story, visit cwmotoracing.com.

www.ingramcontent.com/pod-product-compliance
Lightning Source LLC
Chambersburg PA
CBHW061601120626
46550CB00004B/1568